FINDING GOD'S PEACE
in Everyday Challenges

100 MEDITATIONS *for* WOMEN

HEIDI BRATTON

Published by The Word Among Us Press
7115 Guilford Road
Frederick, Maryland 21704
www.wau.org

19 18 17 16 15   1 2 3 4 5

ISBN: 978-1-59325-278-6
eISBN: 978-1-59325-471-1

Unless otherwise noted, Scripture quotations are from The Holy Bible, English Standard Version® (ESV®), copyright © 2001 by Crossway, a publishing ministry of Good News Publishers. Used by permission. All rights reserved.

Cover design by Koechel Peterson & Associates
Inside photos by Heidi Bratton

Made and printed in the United States of America
Library of Congress Control Number: 2015946178

To my dad, Don Egan, for a childhood filled with nature and unconditional love. Thank you for breaking the chain and overcoming such odds. See you in glory!

To my mom, Carolyn Egan, for a childhood filled with beauty and unconditional support. Thank you for hanging in there to the very end.

I love you and like you both.

ACKNOWLEDGMENTS

Of course, I should have expected a firestorm of conflict when I agreed to write a book on the virtue of peace; every project worth its salt has a laboratory section to go along with it, right? Whether it was in spite of or because of that oversight, writing this book has shown me that there is nothing quite as convincing as a trial by fire and that Jesus Christ really, truly is our peace. So to my dear peace-loving husband, John, thank you for not only sticking with me on this one, but for also pulling me out of the fire on several occasions. I love you always and am ready for that weekend trip, now. Let's go!

Behind every good author is a really great editor, and this book is no exception. Thank you to my incredibly empowering editor, Patty Mitchell! It is a joy to work with you. Thank you also to Jeanne Kun for graciously following through on a chance meeting. I appreciate you! To my most encouraging author/comrade in arms, Lisa Hendey, and to the strong women in my inner circle of support, I am personally indebted to you and buoyed up by your faith daily. Thank you, Nicole, Olivia, Lucy, Marie, Karen, Amy, Jennifer, Diane, Greta, Yvonne, Molly, Teresa, Lisa, Theresa, Debbie, Birgit, Anne,

Pam, Barb, Heidi, Peg, Betsy, and Sr. Maria Faustina. To each of the women who have shared their stories of finding peace in the midst of everyday challenges, thank you for your transparency and trust in sharing those stories. Thank you, most of all, for helping other women to know that they are not alone in seeking to know the peace of our Lord Jesus amid the ups and downs of everyday life.

Contents

INTRODUCTION

"So, what's your new book about, Mommy?" my six-year-old son inquired as he bounded into my home office.

"Well, hello, little man," I answered, surprised that he had escaped from his father's careful watch. "My new book is about peace. Do you know what that is?"

"Nope," he replied, swinging off the back of my office chair, trying to twirl it—and me—away from my computer.

I paused, thinking how to put peace in terms that a six-year-old could grasp. "Well, peace is when someone is not hurried and not worried," I said, and then, seeing that no bells were going off in his head, I added, "Like when you and I finish our chores, and you are not hanging off my chair, and we have all afternoon to swim at the lake." He pondered that for a minute, hopped onto my lap and, looking at me with wide eyes, whispered, "Are you like that, Mommy? Are you not hurried or worried?"

I hugged his innocent little self and didn't know whether to laugh or cry. His question was so sweet and sincere. Was I not hurried or worried? Was I at peace? Should my answer reflect how I was feeling in this exact

moment or in general? Of course, he wouldn't understand the difference, so I went for the truest big-picture
answer.

"I am," I whispered back. "Because God is so good,
Mommy is not hurried nor worried, my little man. I
am at peace because I am holding on to Jesus with
both of my hands!"

In reality, no matter how much we desire peace
and want to be peacemakers, hurry, worry, and all
sorts of big and little skirmishes get in our way. Peace
is not a steady state of being but a dance with time,
stress, conflict, money, misunderstanding, sorrow, and
even outright evil. The real question is not "Are we
at peace?" but "Can holding on tightly to Jesus, the
Prince of Peace, keep us steady on our feet, even when
forces to the contrary try to send us twirling in unexpected circles?"

The very first piece of good news that I bring to you
in this book is "Yes!" For those who embrace the peace
of Jesus Christ, remaining steady on the dance floor
of life is not only possible but to be expected. And I'm
not talking about the slender, kid-friendly definition of
peace that I gave to my son, or an ethereal definition of
peace that wafts through the imaginations of dreamers,
poets, and songwriters. I'm talking about a boundless

yet grounded definition of peace that is lived out in our everyday actions. Peace, as it turns out, is possible and is real because it comes straight from the Lord Jesus, who is our peace (Ephesians 2:14).

Does this seem a little unbelievable in a world of alarming headlines and frequent claims to the contrary? Maybe. But if we look to the family of faith—from biblical heroes to the lives of the saints and even to our fellow believers—we find continuous testimony to the truth that God desires to give his people peace. In both miraculous and mundane ways, the God of peace and grace and blessings moves among us, allowing peace to triumph in the midst of everyday challenges.

I pray that these meditations will introduce you to the stabilizing peace of Jesus Christ. May they help you quiet your heart and open your ears to his comforting words of peace. I pray they will provide you with a few new ways to let the peace of Christ reign in your life and help you live with less hurry and worry. Above all, I pray that you come to a fuller understanding and appreciation of St. Paul's words to the believers in Philippi:

Rejoice in the Lord always; again I will say, rejoice.
Let your reasonableness be known to everyone.

The Lord is at hand; do not be anxious about anything, but in everything by prayer and supplication with thanksgiving let your requests be made known to God. And the peace of God, which surpasses all understanding, will guard your hearts and your minds in Christ Jesus.

Finally, brothers, whatever is true, whatever is honorable, whatever is just, whatever is pure, whatever is lovely, whatever is commendable, if there is any excellence, if there is anything worthy of praise, think about these things. What you have learned and received and heard and seen in me—practice these things, and the God of peace will be with you. (Philippians 4:4-9)

So, dear reader, welcome to these meditations on finding God's peace. Welcome to learning some new and more grace-filled steps in your dance with everyday challenges.

Heidi Bratton

Unconditional Love

Experiences of beauty are one way for us to understand just how unconditional God's love really is. Take the beauty of a sunset, for example. Sunsets are beautiful whether or not someone is there to appreciate them. God's unconditional love is like that. It exists whether or not we accept it, deserve it, or appreciate it.

Practically speaking, this means that Jesus loves us beyond our behavior. It means that he loves us while full well knowing our past, understanding all of our ongoing temptations to sin, and recognizing that no matter how sincere our efforts, perfection is not in our earthly future. It sounds somewhat unbelievable for this type of love to exist, but Scripture tells us that it does: "But God shows his love for us in that while we were still sinners, Christ died for us" (Romans 5:8).

The interesting thing is that in loving us unconditionally, Jesus did not also throw out his standard of perfection. In the Sermon on the Mount, Jesus says this regarding the Ten Commandments: "Do not think that I [Love] have come to abolish the Law or the Prophets; I have not come to abolish them but to fulfill them. For truly, I say to you, until heaven and earth pass away, not an iota, not a dot, will pass from the Law until all is accomplished" (Matthew 5:17-18). Instead of lowering the bar of perfection, however, through his life, death, and resurrection, Jesus gave us the lift that we need to get over the bar. How awe inspiring, uplifting, and peace-filled is that!

It is not always easy to understand, much less accept, this type of unconditional love. Many of us have the illusion that we have to reach perfection, or at least be working very hard to reach it, before we can be deserving of such love. But such thinking is pure rubbish—it really is! You are accepted, loved, and loveable simply because you are a daughter of God, a delight for his eyes to behold.

Lord Jesus, you are my peace. Help me to experience your unconditional and peace-filled love for me.

Breaking Out of the Isolation

Everyday life has a way of isolating us from God. Although I certainly don't mean to put God on the back burner, I can easily get swept up and away from him because of my general busyness. All manner of activities and objects vie for my affection (and my pocketbook). And, yes, even my love for my family can get in the way of my keeping the first commandment: "I am the LORD your God, who brought you out of the land of Egypt, out of the house of slavery. You shall have no other gods before me" (Exodus 20:1–3).

Perhaps you have never thought of busyness or of something as honorable as devotion to your family as a false god, but anything that becomes more important to us than our relationship with God becomes a type of idol, or false god, and over time it will rob us of our peace.

So what does keeping the first commandment look like in the life of a modern woman?

Thankfully, it can take on many forms. For some, putting God first has the very traditional look of attending daily Mass. Other women put God first and stay in sync with the Church by rhythmically praying the

Liturgy of the Hours, the Angelus at noon, or the Divine Mercy Chaplet at three o'clock in the afternoon. For others, putting God first looks like reading Scripture daily, meeting with a Bible-study group weekly, or assisting at Mass on Sundays. One of my favorite ways of opening my heart to God each morning is to sing seasonally appropriate hymns with the family, either around the breakfast table or in the car on the way to school, and again before going to bed at night.

The common ingredient for all of these is that they are not programs or projects; they are simply ways to keep God in the forefront of our lives. Whether through traditional or newer prayers and devotions, we achieve lasting inner peace by continually putting ourselves in God's presence and allowing his love to stabilize our souls.

Lord Jesus, you are my peace. Fill me with the desire to put you first in my life and the discipline to keep you there.

Friendship with Jesus

Renowned poet Maya Angelou once wrote, "I've learned that people will forget what you said, people will forget what you did, but people will never forget how you made them feel."[1]

When I reflect on my life, this statement certainly rings true. To this very day, I can think of people in my life, such as teachers and bosses, who provided me with love and encouragement. Just the memory of their friendships lifts me up, calms me down, refreshes my strength, or restores my peace, depending on what is going on in my life at the time. I feel the same way when I reflect on my friendship with Jesus.

How does reflecting on your journey of faith, your friendship with Jesus, make you feel? I pray that your feelings are those of peace and love and not of anxiety and guilt. But if that's not the case, then Pope Francis has some hopeful words just for you:

When preaching is faithful to the gospel, the centrality of certain truths is evident, and it becomes clear that Christian morality is not a form of stoicism, or self-denial, or merely a practical philosophy or a catalog of sins and faults. Before all else, the gospel invites us to respond to the God of love who saves us, to see God in others, and to go forth from ourselves to seek the good of others. . . .

Everyone needs to be touched by the comfort and attraction of God's saving love, which is mysteriously at work in each person, above and beyond their faults and failings.[2]

It is God's intention that you and I feel his love and know his peace, no matter what we may have heard to the contrary. In the end, our Catholic faith does not boil down to diligent rule keeping. Rather, we are called to generously respond to the love of God by loving him back through prayer and by seeking to share his love with others.

Lord Jesus, you are my peace. Starting today, enkindle or renew my experience of your friendship so that I may experience your saving love and feel your peace.

Doing the Impossible Is Not Our Job

I routinely have to remind myself that I am not Super-woman, much less God. That's obvious, of course, but I'll bet that 99 percent of us women forget this fact as we wake up, throw on our clothes, and fly through our days with impossibly loaded "to-do" lists. Maybe we have all secretly enjoyed being called "Superwoman" at one time or another. But when we come up against the impossible, no cape in the world can help us.

One especially busy fall, my daughter posted this on my Facebook page: "Start by doing what's necessary, then do what's possible, and suddenly you are doing the impossible." That saying, attributed to St. Francis of Assisi, woke me up like a bucket of ice water.

First, it was shocking to realize just how well my child knew me. Second, it was as if my need to achieve the impossible was completely washed away. Here's why.

Even on my toughest days and with the toughest people in my life, I can normally do what is necessary. I need to praise God more than I do for this very basic ability. Doing what is possible, thanks be to God, is also routinely achievable so long as I remain in the sacraments, in God's word, and in fellowship with other Christians.

However, when I hit upon the need to do what I know is impossible, my natural response is to panic. But then I suddenly realize that even if the impossible needs to be done, I am not responsible for getting it done. God is!

Trusting that some of the good things that I want to get done can really only be accomplished by God, who I am not, and on his timetable and in his divine manner, which I cannot know, I am able to peacefully begin to do what is necessary. Then I can move on to what is possible, leaving what is miraculous entirely in God's hands.

Lord Jesus, you are my peace. Help me today to do what is necessary, attempt what is possible, and trust you with the impossible.

The Joy of the Lord

In an era of increasing secularization, I have been questioning whether it is possible to live the Catholic faith in a way that is authentic but also peaceful and attractive to nonbelievers. In other words, how do we share the good news without continually ending up in moral or legalistic arguments?

In his apostolic exhortation *The Joy of the Gospel*, Pope Francis comes to our aid and writes this: "I never tire of repeating those words of Benedict XVI which take us to the very heart of the gospel: 'Being a Christian is not the result of an ethical choice or a lofty idea, but the encounter with an event, a person, which gives life a new horizon and a decisive direction.'"

Pope Francis also quotes from the encyclical *Evangelii Nuntiandi* by Pope Paul VI: "And may the world of our time, which is searching, sometimes with anguish, sometimes with hope, be enabled to receive the good news not from evangelizers who are dejected, discouraged, impatient or anxious, but from ministers of the gospel whose lives glow with fervor, who have first received the joy of Christ."[3]

Pope Francis reminds us that although a saving faith must be solidly grounded in the teachings of the Bible and the Catholic Church, these are not the starting points for anyone, including ourselves, for coming to belief in Jesus. And that is good news when we fear that our efforts to evangelize someone will be filled with conflict.

A faith that is authentic, peaceful, and attractive does not introduce itself remotely through rules and regulations but intimately through love and joy. It is neither caught up in nor brought down by argument. Such a faith, while not avoiding the commandments of the Lord, does not allow these to replace sharing the joy and peace of having encountered the risen Lord Jesus.

I guess the answer to my question of how to peaceably share the good news is found in asking how long it has been since I have encountered the Lord myself. If it has been too long, there is a good chance that my attempts at evangelizing will be marked by unnecessary tension.

Lord Jesus, you are my peace. Open my heart to encounter you and to joyfully and peaceably share that encounter with others.

Sharing the Wonder

I have a friend, Kathleen, who humorously shared this snippet about her life's journey. "So there I was leaping up the corporate ladder, when my biological clock went off. Trust me, I hadn't set the thing, and I really didn't even know I had one! Married and immersed in my career, I hadn't thought that I needed children to be happy, and neither had my husband. But after we had our first child, I looked at my sisters and sisters-in-law and asked them, 'Why didn't you tell me how wonderful motherhood would be? I had no idea what I was missing!'"

Listening to Kathleen, I had to wonder, "What would I say if, after not sharing my faith with someone, that person came to know Jesus and then returned to me and asked, 'Why didn't you tell me how wonderful a relationship with Jesus could be?'" My honest answer would probably boil down to the fact that I had simply been avoiding conflict. When a friend gives the impression that she is "all set" with her condition in life, it's pretty easy for me to be more concerned about keeping the peace of our friendship than with the truth that no one can be "all set" without knowing Jesus (see John 14:6).

When I forget that I am God's messenger, it becomes too easy for me to hide behind my fear of possible conflict or rejection and miss those opportunities to share my faith. In such cases, "keeping the peace" is not a good thing but just another way of not trusting Jesus with my friendships. Remembering, however, that sharing the good news is about helping a friend to have a relationship with Jesus, not with me, helps me share more openly, even with friends who seem to be "all set."

And there is something else too. Jesus has not left us on our own to share the good news. He promised, "But the Helper, the Holy Spirit, whom the Father will send in my name, he will teach you all things and bring to your remembrance all that I have said to you" (John 14:26). Leaning on the Holy Spirit, we can have peace while sharing the wonder of God's salvation.

Lord Jesus, you are my peace. Help me to share your wonderful love and heavenbound peace even with those who appear not to need it.

Finding the Antidote to Stress

Are you "too blessed to be stressed"? That's a popular saying that can be found on coffee mugs and other paraphernalia. And while it's a pithy phrase that also rhymes, I wonder if, on some level, it is encouraging denial rather than consciousness of our circumstances.

Now don't get me wrong—I love the gratitude part of the saying. Remembering our blessings is a truly effective antidote to the poison of stress. However, the antidote (counting our blessings) cannot be entirely effective if we ignore the specific stressful circumstances that are actually poisoning our peace of body, mind, and spirit.

Borrowing from the world of medicine, we see that antidotes are not universal. Antivenoms, for example, are developed to counter venoms from specific snakes, spiders, or other critters. That means that properly identifying the specific venomous creature that bit or stung someone substantially increases that person's chance of getting the right antidote and surviving the unfortunate encounter.

Have you tried being generally prayerful, but it just hasn't brought you more peace? How about being more specific? Does that help? What, exactly, is stressing you out in this chapter of your life? Are you worried about an undiagnosed condition? Are you facing job uncertainty? Are there specific behaviors by specific people that repeatedly trigger your stress?

Identifying rather than denying a specific stress allows us to ask God to provide the specific antidote to it. We can also ask God to help us see the unexpected upsides of the circumstance or to recall the blessings and not just the troubles that seem to come with, for example, a difficult relationship. The more specific we can be in praying for God's help with what is robbing us of our peace, the more capable we will be of recognizing his specific answers. Peace begins with unblinking acknowledgment of the stress at hand and is nurtured by the humility and courage to deal with it.

Lord Jesus, you are my peace. Help me to acknowledge as real that which is robbing me of your peace, be it as small as a cluttered desk or as large as a broken relationship.

A Good Kick in the Shins

A good friend of mine, Debbie, shared with me a profound moment in which God gave her clarity about who she is and, with it, a great sense of peace.

"Growing up, and even into adulthood, my relationship with my mom was somewhat difficult. As a child, I experienced her as emotionally distant and unpredictable; I didn't understand that her tendency to withdraw or withhold her affection had nothing to do with me. When I got married, I struggled with a fear that I would turn out 'just like my mom' and be unable to express love in a healthy and consistent way to my future children.

"Before long, I was immersed in motherhood, facing the everyday challenges of caring for two children born twenty-one months apart. I began to notice a pattern setting in that worried me. More often than I cared to admit, I found myself listening to and believing the lie that as a mother, I was destined to 'inherit' my mom's dysfunction. It became like a self-fulfilling prophecy, affecting my behavior toward my toddlers.

"One afternoon my three-year-old son came into the living room with the evidence of a picture frame he had just broken in two. In my mind, I added it to the long list of ways he had wreaked havoc on our home by his boisterous behavior. As I bent down to take the frame away from him, he kicked me in the shins and ran away laughing. More than anger, I felt an inordinate sense of rejection from my young son, and my immediate response was to be distant, to withdraw from him emotionally.

"Suddenly, there was another voice in my head, not one of condemnation, but one of encouragement and affirmation. Clearly and distinctly, God said to me, 'You are not your mother!' Hearing those words was a defining moment in my life. The truth about who I was, and who I could be with God's help, brought me a tremendous sense of peace, joy, and confidence. As the years went by and our family continued to grow, whenever I was tempted to believe that lie, I clung to those words. I know that moment in my living room helped me become a better, more loving mother."

Lord Jesus, you are my peace. Grant me the peace that comes with believing that I am uniquely me, and no one else.

The Courage That Brings Peace

Sometimes peace is spelled c-o-u-r-a-g-e, as Michelle discovered. "I was at the bedside of my grandfather when he was dying," she said. "I am usually a quiet person, but I turned to everyone in his room, some of whom were Catholic but hadn't been to Mass in years, and asked them to pray with me. It was not easy for me to ask, but I knew it was important for my grandfather's soul. Because it was 3:00 p.m., I taught them the responses to the Divine Mercy Chaplet.

"After we finished, Papa breathed his last breath. He had a peaceful death surrounded by those who loved him and were praying for him. Although I was missing him, I was filled with the strength of God's grace to be peaceful, and people actually commented to my grandma in the nursing home and at the wake, funeral, and reception on how 'beautiful' I looked. I am confident that it was God's gaze they were seeing through me."

Michelle could have prayed the Chaplet in silence, but by courageously asking others to join her in praying, God was able to radiate his gift of peace through and beyond her.

Michelle also showed the kind of courage that bears witness to God's peace in the face of daunting circumstances during the birth of her fourth child.

"I hadn't slept all night, but I was still in the early stages of labor, so I knew it was going to be a long journey. I am a person who needs her sleep, especially when facing something as physically demanding as childbirth. So while I was sitting in the rocking chair in the birthing center, I closed my eyes, prayed, and asked for strength and intervention from St. Gerard, St. Faustina, and Our Blessed Mother. Then I united myself with Jesus spiritually in the Eucharist.

"When I finished, I opened my eyes and the midwife said to me, 'You looked so peaceful. I've never seen a person look so peaceful before. It was so beautiful.' I know it was God's grace in action and the presence of the Trinity in my soul that she was seeing."

Lord Jesus, you are my peace. Help me to have the courage to pray openly and with confidence, no matter what circumstance I may be facing.

Flower Bombing

I spent a frustrating Tuesday staring at the blinking space bar on my computer screen. I was up against a deadline, but everything I was writing seemed so flat and uninspired. It should have been a creative and productive day: it was warm and sunny outside, I had prayed that morning, and my husband had even given me extra time by driving our youngest to school. So why couldn't I write?

Wednesday morning also dawned warm and sunny. Once again I made the same preparations for my workday, but this time I thought I'd warm up to writing by going online first. As I was scrolling through my Facebook news feed, I thought, "There is so much that is alarmist or negative here. I should post something cheerful or positive for my friends." Still not feeling particularly clever (or I would have been writing for my deadline), I decided I should "flower bomb" them by posting photographs of flowers on all of my friends' Facebook walls.

Not more than a half hour later, I had taken photos of some gorgeous pink-tipped roses growing outside my window and posted them along with a short note of encouragement. And when I went back to my writing—what a difference! I felt so much more alive than I had the day before that it was hard to get my fingers to keep pace with the thoughts that flowed through my mind.

Sometimes we want peace in the same way that I wanted to write a fabulous article in one sitting—we want it at our command, and we want it the first time we ask for it. But like the process of creating good literature, art, or music, peace usually can't be forced.

Peace, instead, often sneaks in the back door while we are focusing our attention away from the sources of our conflict or stress and onto activities that are positive, constructive, or creative. Even when we desire peace more than anything else, we must realize that it may take both time and the active pursuit of goodness in other areas of our lives for that sense of peace to come to fruition.

Lord Jesus, you are my peace. Help me to focus my attention on doing good for someone else, all the while trusting that peace will blossom in my life as a result, and in its own sweet time.

In Defense of the Truth

The truth is like a lion.
You don't have to defend it.
Let it loose.
It will defend itself.

I don't know about you, but before reading this quote, I hadn't thought of the truth as being anything like a lion. Candidly, I'd have to say that I had probably treated the truth more like a newborn orphaned koala bear. That is to say, until I encountered this saying (attributed to St. Augustine), I believed that the truth was in urgent need of my protection.

Consequently, when I heard something false, my mode of operation was to rush in and attempt to defend the truth by hitting people over the head with logic, spitting out clever rebuttals, or presenting well-researched, savvy arguments. Alas, none of these approaches resulted in people rolling over and believing the truth. But they did cause a very untidy amount of conflict, which is why I am now so attracted to the idea of letting the truth defend itself.

Adopting such an approach allows us to seek to live in peace even with those who do not accept the truth of the Christian faith or any truth in general. We can be sad for those whose lives are not based on truth and who consequently bear the scars of such lives, but we do not have to constantly point out the scars, nor their origins.

While we always have the responsibility to speak the truth in love, the defense of that truth can be placed squarely in the hands of him who called himself "the way, and the truth, and the life" (John 14:6), the One who is also called the "Lion of Judah" (cf. Revelation 5:5).

When we extend mercy even to those who would try to twist or misuse the truth, peace is the result. We can speak the truth in love calmly and courageously, without resorting to yelling or making a fuss, because as Jesus assures us, the Holy Spirit can convict the hearts of those who have not yet accepted the truth (John 16:8-11).

Lord Jesus, you are my peace. Help me to trust that you are the way, the truth, and the life, and that you can defend yourself.

Finding Peaceful Places

I am not a big-city person. I jokingly tell my kids whenever we visit a big city that I am grateful for all the people who keep the gorgeous museums and grand cathedrals up and running so that we can just drop by for a visit and then go home. Other people I know are just the opposite, finding themselves very much at home in urban settings, not rural ones.

In college I remember laughing when a friend told me that she was so afraid of bears that she could not go hiking in the woods. I shouldn't have laughed; I had an opposite but equally irrational fear of muggers, and I'm sure it kept me from exploring some beautiful areas in different cities.

For each of us, there will be settings and surrounding in which we feel more naturally at home and more peaceful, and we would do well to listen to these feelings. If stress and tension are constant undercurrents in our daily lives, we need to seek out and frequent peaceful places.

Even when my husband and I lived in densely populated graduate-student housing in Berkeley, California, I could get my daily dose of nature by taking a run up a nearby hill and taking in the sweeping view of San Francisco Bay. There were just a few more trees on that hill than if I had run on the city streets below, and the vegetation quieted the city noise, if only slightly. Even though I had not really trekked into the wilderness, when I returned to our apartment, I found that I could better handle the inner-city feel of our housing complex. I also discovered an amazing urban space called a public park! I know it's laughable, but now that we again live in a semi-rural place, I miss those spacious, beautifully manicured parks.

Try taking a "peace inventory." In what places are you most at peace? Are you a city or a country mouse? If you could go anywhere in the world to enjoy a little peace, where would you go, and why? Then ask yourself where you could find such a place close by that would give you that same sense of peace. Make it a point to visit there from time to time.

Lord Jesus, you are my peace. Help me to seek out and frequent places that bring me peace.

The Power of Our Prayers

My young son and I enjoy playing by a little stream near our house. One pleasant afternoon, his little wooden boat (actually just a disk of wood) got stuck on top of a large flat rock in the stream. Not missing a beat, he grabbed a stick and reached way over the water trying to dislodge it with the stick. Unfortunately, his stick was too short. Reaching out just a little too far, he lost his balance and fell into the stream hands first.

Amazingly, the slight change in water level and the redirecting of water currents from his hands thrusting into the water were just enough to lift his boat off the rock and set it free. Without ever touching the boat, my son's actions freed the boat from being snagged and allowed it to continue on its way downstream.

Watching this scene unfold from the opposite side of the stream, I suddenly understood the effects of intercessory prayer. As it was with my son and his stick, oftentimes it is beyond our reach to give direct help to someone who has run into a snag in life. However, in some mystical way God has set up the spiritual realm like a body of water. Our diving into the water with prayers, petitions, praises, and sacrifices changes the course of the spiritual currents, effecting change for those who need help by bringing God's peace into stressful or chaotic situations.

Imagine someone doing a cannonball into a backyard pool. Everything floating in the pool is affected by the waves and the rise in water level. In a lighthearted way, we could call intercessory prayer a "spiritual cannonball" and understand why it is that the more often we "jump" (pray), the better. All the more reason to "jump" higher and harder!

When I begin to doubt the effectiveness of intercessory prayer, I recall my son's falling in the stream and how it set his little boat free. Then I resolve to do some spiritual cannonballs!

Lord Jesus, you are my peace. Help me to delight in knowing that prayer works! Remind me to do "spiritual cannonballs" for peace in the world, in my community, in my home, and in my heart.

Of Seagulls and Rain

To raise funds for our children's Catholic high school, we join with several hundred volunteers after home games on Sunday mornings to clean the University of Michigan's football stadium—the largest in the country, with an official capacity of more than 109,000 people.

The first time I walked into that trash-covered stadium, I was totally overwhelmed. I looked at bleachers covered with spilled nachos, scattered popcorn kernels, abandoned water bottles, and clingy yellow pom-pom tassels, and I thought, "There's no way. This is impossible!"

I picked up my little broom at the stadium gates, and the attendant told me to follow after those raking up the garbage and to be sure to check for gunk stuck under the bleachers. I took my job seriously—too seriously, as it turned out, because at one point a more experienced volunteer impatiently mentioned, "Really, it's okay to leave some popcorn behind." I barely looked up at him, righteously thinking, "That's not what the attendant told me!"

After the stadium was cleaned, we assembled for Mass in one section of the bleachers. That first morning

I was shocked to see great swirling flocks of seagulls descending on the stadium, consuming anything that was remotely edible. Then, as we carefully processed down the steep bleacher stairs for Communion, it started to rain. "Oh," I humbly thought, "the attendant didn't mention that there would be acts of God like seagulls and rain to help with the cleanup!"

Can we believe that a vast majority of the ways in which peace will come to our homes, our communities, and our world is completely out of our hands but entirely in God's? Can we do our part and have peace that our God, who is able to send seagulls and rain to finish the job, is the One who is really in charge?

Lord Jesus, you are my peace. Help me to faithfully do my small part for the work of peace, trusting that you've got the bigger picture well in hand.

More Love, Less Duty

One day when I was alone at daily Mass, I became especially conscious of the celebrant as he cleared the altar after Communion. As the sounds of a meditative hymn floated down from the choir loft, he carefully placed the ciborium full of blessed hosts back in the tabernacle, lovingly wiped the chalice, and neatly folded the altar cloths.

He was in no hurry.

His disposition was so deliberately loving and peaceful that it was clear that he was not thinking of cleaning up as some kind of necessary evil to rush through so that he could get on with the rest of the Mass. In fact, I got the impression that he had completely forgotten that we were still in the church with him!

So I asked myself, "What would change in our house if I cleaned up after dinner with more love and less duty, like the priest cleaning up after the Lord's Supper? Is it possible that the emotional atmosphere might become more peaceful, like that of this Mass? Of course, I don't have this lovely choir in my home, and the priest does not have children to get ready for bed. But what if there were more poise and less frenzy radiating from me after meals? What if I put on some high-quality music? Might not the whole family experience more peace?"

Still transfixed by the activity taking place on the altar, I watched as the priest gathered the chalice, the altar cloths, and the tabernacle keys and reverently handed them to his two altar servers. The two young men, whom I personally know to be pretty mischievous middle-school boys, accepted the items, bowed, and calmly carried them off the altar.

"It's true," I had to conclude. "Change your attitude, change your atmosphere." The priest's poise and peacefulness set the stage for the entire atmosphere of the Mass.

Which everyday tasks could be transformed by a change in your attitude, thereby bringing a more peaceful atmosphere to your home? Doing the laundry? Paying the bills? Taking the dog to the vet?

Lord Jesus, you are my peace. Give me the grace to do all my work with less duty and more love as I seek to bring peace into my home.

Change Is Possible

Sometimes all we need to do in order to have more peace in life is to bear in mind that no matter what we are dealing with, change is possible. I was reminded of this truth after dealing with our six-year-old son, who had a pretty rough entry into first grade. The first few weeks of school were a roller coaster of tears, fits, and previously unseen direct disobedience. At one point, I thought he just might be grounded for the rest of his natural-born life!

Then one morning, for reasons I cannot explain, he had the perfect first-grade day. I woke him up and he got out of bed. No fits, no tears, no diving back under the covers. When I returned from making breakfast, I was awed by the sight of his little fingers trying to button up his school uniform all by himself. No wrestling match to get him dressed. Peace reigned in our house that morning! Even at bedtime, there were no tears as he sang in his shower, jumped into his pajamas, and plopped into bed for prayers. I left his room that night thinking, "Wow—it's true! Nothing is impossible with God!"

As I continually seek to live a more peace-filled life, seeing my son's behavior turn such a positive corner so abruptly and with no direct aid from me was a good reminder to have more patience with people—including myself—because change is possible. It just may take more time than I want it to take.

We hear many voices—perhaps coming from the latest study on the brain or on genetics—that say change is not possible. But change is possible. It might be a natural change that happens with maturity, or a difficult change that requires therapy, or a good old-fashioned decision to change one's habits. It could even be a straight-up miracle. In response to the question of who could be saved, Jesus said this to his disciples: "With man this is impossible, but with God all things are possible" (Matthew 19:26).

What seemingly impossible things do you need changed in order to have more daily peace? Let them be known to God, with whom all things are possible, and then wait and act in hope.

Lord Jesus, you are my peace. Help me hold on to the truth that change is possible.

Breaking through That Wall

Do you ever go into perpetual avoidance mode? You know what you ought to be doing, but you find it just too hard, or too uncomfortable, or too expensive (or whatever excuse comes to mind). So you just wall off your thoughts and emotions about it.

Reconciling the monthly budget and cleaning the kitty litter box are two such small things that I routinely try to lock behind ten-foot thick concrete walls. I just can't manufacture the desire to do them, mostly because they are never completely done. But when they are not kept up-to-date, I am either haunted by the fear of overdrawing the bank account or by a noxious odor stealthily moving through the house. Although I know the value of doing these two chores, I still must make an act of the will to get them done. When I do, however, the resulting feelings are always the same: relief and freedom, like a bird flying out of its cage.

Getting to the Sacrament of Confession is like that. It often takes an act of the will for me to get there. It's not that I don't know that I've sinned or that sin is adding unresolved conflict to my life. I do know. And it's not that I haven't experienced the incredible relief and freedom of forgiveness and absolution. I have. It's just that standing between me and the confessional is a ten-foot thick wall of effort called getting out the door at the right time and not letting something else more "urgent" get ahead of it.

Catholic author Matthew Kelly shares this idea about getting over the activation hurdle of going to Confession: "Our lives change when our habits change. . . . I learned that I have to pick a specific time [to go to Confession] each month. Otherwise, one month started turning into two or three. That way, there is no confusion, and I don't open the door to procrastination, laziness, and all those other lurking traits that want to steal me away from God and my best self."[4]

Lord Jesus, you are my peace. Help me over the hurdles of getting to Confession so that I might experience the relief and freedom of being forgiven.

An Hour of Peace

"Come to me, all who labor and are heavy laden, and I will give you rest" (Matthew 11:28). Have you ever heard a more beautiful command followed by an even more beautiful promise? What woman hasn't craved just five minutes of rest?

My friend Karen, a mother with three children, shares how she finally learned to experience the rest the Lord promises.

"After we joined a new parish, I thought we should do our part to support the Adoration program there. The first fall that our two oldest children were in preschool, my husband agreed to watch the baby while I covered an hour of Adoration. I am sure I had gone to Adoration during my Catholic school years, but I really had never gone on purpose, and certainly not for an hour! So there I was, not really ever having had a break from the kids since my oldest was born, taking my only hour off to 'babysit' Jesus.

"I spent the first hour getting really worked up about all the things I should be getting done with an hour alone. I just couldn't believe how stressed I was becoming with all that time to think. I would like to report that by the following week, I had reoriented myself to the point of knowing why I was there and loving my time with Jesus, but that was not the case. Fortunately, I had signed up for this hour of Adoration pretty much forever, so in time I started giving over my stresses to Jesus, placing them at the foot of the cross. By the time school was out that spring, Adoration was my hour of peace. Over the years, my hour in Adoration has become my hour to rest in the midst of family life."

The Scripture passage above from the Gospel of Matthew continues in this way: "Take my yoke upon you, and learn from me, for I am gentle and lowly in heart, and you will find rest for your souls. For my yoke is easy, and my burden is light" (11:29-30). Using Karen's example, let's place ourselves in the presence of Jesus more and more so that we, too, may find rest for our souls.

Lord Jesus, you are my peace. Guide me as I seek to find my rest in you.

Abandoning Our Burdens to the Lord

Hannah, a woman in the Old Testament, is an excellent role model for how to get real with God as we try to carry the burdens that are robbing us of Christ's peace.

Hannah was one of Elkanah's two wives. Because of her childlessness, Hannah was taunted by Elkanah's other wife. Although Elkanah tried to comfort Hannah with his love and provision, Hannah was miserable, weepy, and did not eat (1 Samuel 1:7).

So what did Hannah do with this all-consuming, peace-stealing grief? One year, during her husband's annual trek to the temple at Shiloh, Hannah went into the temple herself for a firsthand encounter with God. So dramatically did she pour out her heart to God that Eli, the priest in attendance, accused her of being drunk!

After Hannah explained the reason for her sadness and told him of her prayer for a child, Eli was convinced that she was not drunk—except with grief. Then he said an amazing thing to her: "Go in peace, and the God of Israel grant your petition that you have made to him" (1 Samuel 1:17). Even more amazing than what Eli said is what Hannah did. She changed her attitude and embraced the peace that Eli had offered her.

Hannah's encounter with God in the temple marks the height of conflict in her life story. To the temple she brings her greatest burden, childlessness, and basically throws it at God's feet. Then without any tangible proof that God will positively answer her prayer, she walks out, leaving her burden behind. Hannah's peace is restored, not because God has yet answered her prayer, but because, with the help of Eli, she has handed her burden to God and trusted him with it.

This is good news for those of us who are carrying great burdens! If we are as authentic with God as Hannah was in presenting our burdens to him and then leave them with God in faith and trust, we also can have the peace that Hannah experienced.

Lord Jesus, you are my peace. Help me to be authentic in my prayers, to abandon my burdens to you, and to be restored to peace, both with you and with my situation.

Emotional Peace

My husband and I had another clash of expectations last night. Who knew that after twenty-five years of marriage, we still wouldn't be able to live in perfect harmony at all times! In today's technological age, shouldn't there be a mind-reading app that we could buy from iHeaven.com?

I keep thinking that after all these years, we should be able to move past certain predictable clashes. But the problem seems to lie in our vastly different emotive personalities. Even with our shared faith and compatible core values and goals, conflicts can still arise because of the different ways in which we emotionally experience, process, and express the daily events of our lives.

Thankfully, for my husband and me, the grace of the Sacrament of Marriage comes to our rescue as many times as our fallen human natures clash. The roller-coaster ride from conflict to resolution is not exactly peaceful, however, so in my quest to shorten and level out the dips and loops of conflict, I have learned two things.

The first is that emotions themselves are morally neutral. Although negative emotions may feel "wrong," it is only the action one takes on any emotion that can be either moral or immoral. I may get angry with my husband, but it is in how I decide to express that anger to him that matters. As well-formed Catholics, we should feel anger at injustice but use that anger as fuel for doing good, like volunteering with the pro-life movement. Jesus used his anger for good when he cleared the temple of the money changers (Luke 19:46).

The second is that being unemotional is not the same as being peaceful, even though being unemotional can look or even temporarily feel like it. However, the goal is not to deny, submerge, or kill our emotions. God created us with emotions, and so obviously we are not to throw them away. In fact, the *Catechism of the Catholic Church* tells us that we should be moved to the good not only by our wills but also by our hearts (1775)—just as Jesus was moved in the temple.

Lord Jesus, you are my peace. Help me to embrace the gift of emotions. Show me how to temper and use all my emotions for good so that I may experience more peace.

The Importance of a Slight Turn

I love road trips. Over the years, I've found a myriad of ways to entertain my six children and myself as we speed along the highway. One of the things that has always fascinated me is highway exit ramps.

An exit ramp begins with the slightest turn (and hopefully a little deceleration). The final trajectory of that slightest turn, however, can range from a minor change of direction, allowing one to gain access to a wayside, to a 180-degree change of direction, allowing one to retrieve that forgotten cell phone left on the kitchen counter.

Imagine the incredible possibilities if one wakes up in Kansas City, Missouri, and decides to drive for twelve hours. Exiting the highway around Kansas City with the four points of the compass, at dinner one could have moose burgers in Winnipeg, Canada, crab cakes in Washington, DC, shrimp gumbo in Port Arthur, Texas, or buffalo steaks in Grand Junction, Colorado. What vastly different places to end up after having started from the same place that morning!

The same thing can happen when we make even the slightest change in our spiritual focus at the beginning of the day. We could park ourselves at the annoying fact that we woke up to the dog's mess on the rug or a traffic jam that made us late for work. Or we could move past those irritations by making even the slightest turn to prayer.

As slight turns at sunrise off the highways around Kansas City will lead to vastly different places by dinner, turning in various degrees to prayer in the morning will result in a vastly different spiritual state—not only by dinnertime, but throughout the day.

Do you want to arrive at a place of spiritual peace at the end of the day? Make a slight change in the direction of your heart and trust God to get you there.

Lord Jesus, you are my peace. Help me to turn my heart toward you and toward your mother, Mary, when difficulties merge into my lane.

Peace with Motherhood

No matter how much we try to ignore it, the secular culture can affect our mind-set about childbearing. Our fertility is one of God's greatest gifts to us women, and yet it is often presented as a curse to be medicated away or to be cut off by surgery. Having children is considered just one of many options for personal self-fulfillment. Children themselves are often thought of as time hogs and financial burdens, more like investments to be managed than individuals to be loved.

And yet, the truth is that the majority of women still have children, which sets up an internal conflict and a lack of peace. A friend of mine, Andrea, shared that even with a strong Christian faith, her perspective on motherhood was skewed.

"With my first three pregnancies, when I realized that I was expecting, I grieved. I was sad about how little time my husband and I would have to enjoy with each other without the stresses of parenting. I grieved my independent lifestyle, my freedom, and my energy. I found childbearing and child rearing to be very restricting, exhausting, and even debilitating. Because I came from a broken and abusive home, a healthy family life was foreign to me, and I did not feel fit for the task of parenting. I struggled deeply because although I love my children, I couldn't help thinking that I would have been able to love them more if they had come later in my marriage and at a much more reasonable pace!"

Thankfully, Andrea went on to share about her change of heart after she experienced a period of infertility and then went on to have three more children. "This Scripture passage has completely enlightened me on my mothering journey: 'Yet she will be saved through childbearing—if they continue in faith and love and holiness, with self-control' (1 Timothy 2:15). This verse is my testimony that as much as I rejected childbearing for worldly reasons and the desires of the flesh, God showed me his love and specific plan for my life through childbearing. The pregnancies have healed me physically, and seeing God's power in my life firsthand has healed me emotionally and spiritually."

Lord Jesus, you are my peace. Help me to view the uniquely feminine gift of fertility as you do, not as the world does.

Getting Help When We Need It

When an agitated extended family member confronted me in an aggressive way this week, I had to call in a third party for help. Can I just say that it was not fun? Nevertheless, and as regrettable as it may be, there are times when involving a third party is the best thing we can do. Someone outside the conflict can help us set boundaries so that we can protect ourselves from unacceptable behavior, thus restoring our peace.

Even today, however, when there is so much help available, there still lingers a kind of embarrassment or shame about involving therapists, social workers, or other professionals in our personal lives. We might erroneously think, "This can't be happening to me, but even if it is, I surely don't want anyone to know about it." Or we might reason, "I'm tough enough to fix this on my own." Worse yet is if we mistakenly think, "It's not 'Christian' to complain or to confront someone about their poor behavior. Christ suffered, so who am I not to suffer?"

God has created each of us with personal dignity, and no one has the right to offend, abuse, or discredit that dignity. My "go-to" piece of biblical advice on the topic comes from Jesus as he instructed his disciples: "And whatever town or village you enter, find out who is worthy in it and stay there until you depart. As you enter the house, greet it. And if the house is worthy, let your peace come upon it, but if it is not worthy, let your peace return to you. And if anyone will not receive you or listen to your words, shake off the dust from your feet when you leave that house or town" (Matthew 10:11-14).

If others have treated you as unworthy for a long time, you may have a hard time "shaking the dust from your feet." Know this, however: peaceably separating yourself from such people is what Jesus advises. Also know that you are worth the spending of whatever resources (time, energy, money, emotion) it may take to reclaim your dignity and restore peace to your life.

Lord Jesus, you are my peace. Help me to know that I am worthy of your love and the love and respect of others. If necessary, give me the strength to get third-party help, and to peaceably walk away from anyone who would try to offend my personal dignity.

"Friending" and "Unfriending"

I finally took the time to reduce the number of "friends" on my personal Facebook account. It took me two hours, but it has already given me so much peace of mind.

On the one hand, the awkward relationships inherent to social media are not new. Human friendships have always been dynamic and punctuated by times of "friending" and "unfriending." Even if we have lived in one place for a long time, we most likely have made new friends and let other friendships fade away. Who hasn't had that embarrassing moment of bumping into an old acquaintance at the grocery store and not remembering her name? And it becomes even more challenging if we have lived in several different places. We will know too many good people to be able to keep in touch with them all.

On the other hand, social media is a complete game changer. The age-old notions of privacy and keeping personal and professional friendships separate have been completely bulldozed by social media, heightening rather than diminishing the tension that naturally arises between different types and levels of friendship.

There is no neutral zone when anytime you go online, someone is either waiting for your next post or tweet or is expecting you to respond to theirs!

In the past, friendships used to wax and wane according to our interests and activities, and some friendships would just naturally fade away. Now we are faced with this moment in time when we have to choose to click a tab that actually says, "Unfriend." It just seems so abrupt and, well, so unfriendly!

For me, the Facebook awkwardness of having friends of differing levels of intimacy from so many different places and times in my life was compounded by also having a professional presence online as a Catholic author and photographer. How to best merge and manage all these friendships in a virtual landscape is still a bit of a mystery to me, but shrinking my personal Facebook account back to personal friends feels like a good, peace-filled start.

Lord Jesus, you are my peace. Help me to navigate social media wisely and to have peace by making conscious decisions about both old and new friendships.

Sowing in Peace

I love how the following Scripture verse places the virtue of peace in an agricultural context: "For where jealousy and selfish ambition exist, there will be disorder and every vile practice. But the wisdom from above is first pure, then peaceable, gentle, open to reason, full of mercy and good fruits, impartial and sincere. And a harvest of righteousness is sown in peace by those who make peace" (James 3:16-18).

By writing in this way, St. James shows us that even if being peace-loving is not always native to our fallen human natures, it is possible to cultivate peace in our lives just as farmers cultivate crops that may not be native to their land.

If you have ever planted even the smallest of gardens, the first thing you discover is that farming at any level is a huge commitment of time and energy. If one wants to harvest a crop, one cannot simply throw seeds on the ground and walk away.

If we look at our spiritual lives through an agricultural lens, we might say that the wisdom from heaven is the seed that needs to be planted in our hearts. The preparation of the soil of our hearts takes place when we faithfully attend to our sacramental lives. Once the soil is ready and wisdom has been sown, we water the seeds with the grace of the Eucharist, Confession, prayer, and Bible reading. We fertilize the wisdom that comes from heaven with corporal and spiritual works of mercy. When we root out from our thinking lies and half-truths, it is as if were weeding our spiritual gardens. Steadfastly seeking to break bad habits that creep into our lives is like applying spiritual pest control.

Corn, wheat, and soybeans—today these are staple crops in the Midwest region of the United States, but they were not native species to every part of the region. What can we do today to make peace, kindness, and mercy the staples of our lives, even if they don't seem to be our "native" qualities?

Lord Jesus, you are my peace. Help me to sow in peace the wisdom that comes from heaven. Help me, also, to nurture that seed of wisdom so that I can reap a harvest of righteousness.

Reconsidering the Rat Race

My father used to comment about the pace of my life as a mother of six by saying, "Gee, Heidi, it sounds to me like you're trying to pack ten pounds of flour into a five-pound sack." Being from a different generation, my dad never really understood the whole carpooling or club-sports part of our family life, but what he did notice and understand was spot on. There is a certain absurdity about the amount of activity that we modern women try to squeeze into every twenty-four-hour period.

As we try to establish a more peaceful pace of life, whether it is with work or family activities, we need to ask ourselves, "Why am I trying to do so much that I am in constant need of more than twenty-four hours a day to get it all done?" To find an answer to this question, it can be useful to step back and examine historical precedent.

Think for a minute about life, not just back when we were kids, but before electricity. Native people all over the globe got up and went to sleep with the rhythm of the sun. Lack of light was their permission to sleep, but today electricity has disrupted that organic rhythm of activity and rest. Consider the irony of our need to carve time out of our schedules in order to get to the gym because so much of our work is sedentary. Native people would really just shake their heads and go back to hoeing their fields or hunting wild game.

The point to consider here is that maybe our lives lack a peaceful pace not because we haven't synchronized our schedules well enough, but because we are really trying to do too much. Comedian Lily Tomlin gave us a humorous nudge toward reexamining the pace of our lives by saying, "The trouble with the rat race is that even if you win, you're still a rat."[5]

Lord Jesus, you are my peace. Help me to step back and reconsider my activity load. Help me to know if I should put some activities on hold for a while and, if so, which ones.

The ABCs of Sharing the Truth

Have you ever noticed how much we hear about tolerance today? It seems to have rocketed to the top of the world's virtue chart, leaving behind in a cloud of smoke the Christian virtue of truth. In fact, it is often said that tolerance, and tolerance alone, is what is needed to bring about world peace. Truth is often considered passé and, ironically, as an intolerable instrument of divisiveness.

As Catholics, we need only read our Bibles to see that truth believed, lived, and shared in love is, in fact, the only way of peace. We know this not only because our Lord called himself "the truth," but also because he told us that "the truth will set [us] free" (John 14:6; 8:32). And although the phrase "instructing the ignorant" is definitely not politically correct, it is the second of the seven spiritual works of mercy and something we must do.

So how do we promote peace by sharing the truth in love in a world in which many are predisposed against it (and maybe against us as well)? I propose we envision ourselves as teachers in a spiritual kindergarten and start with the basics. First we look at our students with love, and then we joyfully do the following in A-B-C order:

Acknowledge each person by listening and desiring to know where he or she is coming from.
Affirm who they are, uniquely created and beloved by God.
Ask sincere questions to clarify what has been said, not assuming that we have understood correctly the first time.

Be prepared to give the reason for the hope that is within us (1 Peter 3:15), not the reason we are right and they are wrong; but the reason we have hope in something different—in Jesus.
Believe that Jesus loves these people more than we do and that he will reveal himself and the truths of Christianity to them.

Correct gently without sarcasm or belittling.

Lord Jesus, you are my peace. Help me to grasp fully, live joyfully, and share confidently the truth of the Catholic faith with nonbelievers.

The Essential Ingredient

Sometimes we miss the essential aspect of something because it isn't a corporal entity. For example, we could mix together every ingredient listed in a cake recipe, but if we did not also put the batter in the oven, we would never have a cake. Heat is the only absolutely essential "ingredient" of all the incredible cakes out there.

Jesus is to a peace-filled life what heat is to the process of producing a cake: the only absolutely essential ingredient. Jesus, however, is not a source of energy, like heat. Jesus is a Person, fully God and fully man, who came down from heaven to have a saving relationship with us. And through the Holy Spirit, he remains on the earth, eager to continue having a saving relationship with us. St. Paul tells us this:

> For he himself is our peace, who has made us both [Jew and Gentile] one and has broken down in his flesh the dividing wall of hostility by abolishing the law of commandments expressed in ordinances, that he might create in himself one new man in place of the two, so making peace, and might reconcile us both to God in one body through the

cross, thereby killing the hostility. And he came and preached peace to you who were far off and peace to those who were near. For through him we both have access in one Spirit to the Father. (Ephesians 2:14-18)

Maybe you've been trying really hard to create and maintain peace in your life, but your heart remains troubled. Maybe you've mixed in all the right ingredients: going to Confession, receiving the Eucharist at Mass, or even offering forgiveness to someone who has hurt you. But maybe you are still missing the main ingredient, because despite your outward actions, you have not yet opened the door of your heart to Jesus.

When asked what was the greatest commandment, Jesus answered, "You shall love the Lord your God with all your heart and with all your soul and with all your strength and with all your mind, and your neighbor as yourself" (Luke 10:27).

In order to know the peace of Christ, we must know Christ first. Everything else depends on this.

Lord Jesus, you are my peace. Help me to know you and open my heart to you.

The Peace of an Organized Home

Okay, I'll admit it. I'm a little compulsive when it comes to keeping the house clean and organized. For example, I have a hard time starting dinner if my countertops are littered with dishes and food from breakfast and lunch. Although I enjoy getting the newspaper on Sunday mornings, by Sunday afternoon I am gathering up the scattered sections and tossing them in the recycling bin because it drives me nuts when they get spread out all over the house.

Neatness is not a virtue I asked to have. It just sort of increased in me as the size of our family also increased. Some women's magazines and online blogs elevate neatness to a moral virtue. I don't think it is, but it is a simple fact that as the "CEO and plant manager" of a large family, I have to budget the time to straighten and clean the house.

Someone once told me, oh so cheerfully, "Don't sweat the small stuff." However, sticky floors and piles of dirty laundry are not small stuff for me. There was a brief period of time when I did try to stay calm and play with my preschoolers while ignoring the mounting chaos. But you know what? It only revealed even more that I prefer "sweating" to living with a mess.

It's easy to resist making it a priority to stay on top of household chores. We can easily rationalize putting it off by thinking that we have to choose between a tidy house or time with our family and friends. But it's not an either/or situation. It's not that I think that cleaning and organizing are more important than reading to my toddler or talking with my teenagers. But when I'm organized, it strengthens and supports my ability to do everything else. Setting priorities and then managing our time well so that we can complete what needs to get done help us stay calm, peaceful, and ready for the next thing that God is calling us to do.

Lord Jesus, you are my peace. Help me to prioritize my time, energy, and talents as I seek to care for the household you have given me.

A Little Thing Called Time

So there's this little thing called procrastination. And time. And managing it. And really, who ever invented clocks anyway?

There are so many temptations for me not to pay attention to the time constraints of the task at hand. As when I'm trying to finish writing this paragraph, but my coffee cup is almost empty, and so maybe I should go brew another cup before really settling down to writing . . . and on and on the story of procrastination goes.

In today's digital world, the word "procrastination" has many different names—like Facebook, or YouTube, or Pinterest, or other websites and mobile phone apps. In such a world, our time-management skills probably have more potential than any other life skill to either give or rob us of peace.

In chapter 9 of the Gospel of John, Jesus is confronted by the religious leaders for healing a man born blind on the Sabbath, a day of the week when work was prohibited by Mosaic law. In defense of his use of this time, Jesus simply says, "We must work the works of him who sent me while it is day; night is coming, when no one can work" (John 9:4). To hone our time-management skills to be like Jesus', perhaps all we need to ask is this: "What is the work God has asked of me, and am I doing it right now?" If yes, carry on. If no, stop *now*, and get back on track.

With regard to keeping us on track, technology can add to our sense of peace when it is used properly. For example, I now use my cell-phone timer the way I had often used the oven timer—to remind me of when someone needs to be picked up from school or even to let my toddler know when his game time is over.

Lord Jesus, you are my peace. Help me to realize how important good time management is to my daily peace. Help me choose not to procrastinate, and please, help me choose it now!

The Snares of the Devil

It is a habit in some parishes to pray the Prayer to Saint Michael the Archangel at the end of each Mass. It is a short but powerful prayer:

St. Michael the Archangel, defend us in battle.
Be our defense against the wickedness and
  snares of the devil.
May God rebuke him, we humbly pray, and
  do thou,
O Prince of the heavenly hosts, by the power
  of God,
thrust into hell Satan, and all the evil spirits,
who prowl about the world seeking the ruin
  of souls.

I especially love two images in this prayer. The word "snares" reminds me that very few of us run around wantonly breaking the Ten Commandments by stealing rampantly or murdering people. And yet we are all sinners. Big temptations to sin are on our radar like bear traps on a hiking path. We can see and usually avoid them. Little temptations to sin are like the snares used for rabbits and skunks. They are covered up by leaves, off to the side, and easily overlooked. Both traps and snares are set for us by the devil, by our own flesh, and by the world. But big or small, no matter what their origin, temptations to sin trip us up on the road to living peaceful, God-fearing lives.

And then there is the second image: "All the evil spirits, who prowl about the world seeking the ruin of souls." This reminds me that our enemy has minions who, like him, do not want us to live in peace. In the same way that the devil doesn't care if I commit a thousand little sins or one big one, as long as I turn my back on God, the devil isn't above having someone else do his dirty work.

I'm not really the warrior type, but saying the Prayer to Saint Michael the Archangel, especially as a congregation in church, really gives me peace. It strengthens my faith and sharpens my desire to stay close to the Lord.

Lord Jesus, you are my peace. Help me to stay alert to the snares of the devil through frequent prayer and the awareness of your power and ability to protect me.

Loved beyond Our Fears

My friend Allison shares a story of a time when she not only received God's peace but also learned a lesson about his faithfulness.

"For six months, as I held onto a photo of the little girl whom we were going to adopt from China, I dreamed of holding her in my arms. When we finally went to the Wuhan consulate to meet her, the initial meeting went very well. Faith seemed receptive to my husband, Kevin, and to me. However, when we returned to the hotel, things changed. Kevin and the Chinese interpreter left to buy her milk and some snacks. The minute the door closed behind Kevin, Faith began to wail—hysterically! She became so inconsolable at being alone with me that she actually threw up.

"For many years, I had prayed for the Blessed Mother to wrap me in her mantle, but until this moment, I had not truly understood what that meant. As I sat there with my new little girl rejecting my every attempt to love her, feeling afraid that she might never accept me as her mother, I was comforted by the presence of my heavenly Mother. I knew that she was watching over me, interceding for me, and loving me.

"The more I prayed, the more my heart was at peace, and I understood that God was teaching me something in the midst of this struggle. I was reminded of my own rejection of God. For many years, God wanted nothing more than to be my loving Father, but I had rejected those advances. Instead of recognizing the gift of his love and care in my life, I had withdrawn in fear and was unwilling to trust him. In doing my 'own thing,' I often found myself crying just as hysterically as Faith had that first afternoon when the door closed."

This child, so desired and already loved by Allison, did not immediately desire or love Allison as her mother. Instead of allowing this to rob her peace, however, Allison was reminded of how faithful God had been to her, and she knew exactly how to become Faith's mother: by staying put.

Lord Jesus, you are my peace. Thank you for choosing me to be your adopted daughter and for never abandoning me.

Building a Spiritual Immune System

I woke up with a sore throat. I can't tell yet whether it's one of those "supervillain" types of bugs that will knock me into bed for a couple of days or one of those "sidekick, clingy" types that will hang on annoyingly for weeks. However, I've already had two glasses of water and a fresh-fruit smoothie to give my immune system the edge I know it's going to need to shake this thing.

As I was going through the trouble of making a fruit smoothie, two things occurred to me. First, why do I wait until I'm feeling poorly to make the time to care for my body? What if I got plenty of rest and ate a vitamin C-rich diet all along? Wouldn't I have a super-heroic immune system and be able to fight off all pesky bugs? And then I thought, "Wow, does this apply to the spiritual life!"

Why do I wait until there is a crisis before "going through the trouble" of making Jesus a part of my life? What if I had a daily prayer time and studied the Bible all along? Wouldn't I be able to fight off those pesky temptations to sin, like gossiping when my co-worker stopped by my office yesterday?

The truth is that if we want to increase our immunity to sins that are both the "supervillain" kind and the "sidekick" type, we need to make time for healthy spiritual behaviors.

When I asked my friend Theresa what brings peace to her life, she said, "Confession, Confession, Confession. I can't tell you how many times I was struggling with guilt, anger, or anxiety, went to Confession, and walked out floating. I always experience a very tangible lifting of my spirits, a clearing of the brain fog, and a deep and profound sense of joy as the priest utters the words of absolution."

Notice that Theresa did not say that her soul was deathly ill with mortal sin. She examined her conscience when she woke up to achy feelings of guilt, anger, and anxiety. Then she gave her spiritual immune system a boost by going to Confession. And she came out of Confession with lifted spirits, brightened thoughts, and abundant joy.

Lord Jesus, you are my peace. Help me to get to Confession and do something today to boost my spiritual immune system.

Baskets Full of Time

Many people comment that we live in a time-starved culture. I know this because comparing schedules and groaning about our busyness is one of the favorite pastimes of us parents chatting about our children's activities. Typically, it is just harmless chatter, but there is something in the chatter that conveys an inaccurate sense of our being helpless victims of time, and this can rob us of our peace.

To better understand that we may not be as time-starved as we imagine, we can think of time as a loaf of bread. At the stroke of midnight of each new day, we each get the same-sized loaf, or twenty-four hours' worth of bread.

Most of us take our loaf of time and begin doling it out to different "baskets" with labels such as "work," "exercise," "carpooling," "kids," "shopping," and so forth. As we divide up our loaves, however, there is a tendency for crumbs to break off, to miss the baskets, and to get wasted. These crumbs have generic names like "distractions" and "procrastination" as well as proper names like "Reality TV" and "YouTube." Quite likely, if we were to gather together all our crumbs of wasted time, they would fill a basket larger than any single one of the others.

In the end, I am convinced that the true availability of our personal resources (our time, money, energy, or any other personal resource) is not as scarce as we often convince ourselves that it is.

My adult son demonstrated this to me when he was preparing for finals at the end of his first semester in law school. Knowing that he was going to need more time than usual to study, he gathered into one digital file all his nonessential cell-phone apps like Facebook and NFL.com. Rather than letting time just crumble away from his twenty-four-hour loaf, my son identified and gathered every last crumb of time and put them in the basket labeled "time to study." It was a great reminder to me to reexamine areas of my life in which I may be frittering away my resources instead of gathering them up and spending them in pursuit of higher goals.

Lord Jesus, you are my peace. Help me to gather all my resources and put them at your disposal, even those that I sometimes fritter away.

Motivation to Get off the Couch

I am a firm believer that an orderly environment lends itself to a peaceful environment, whether it is at home, church, or the workplace. However, sometimes I need a little motivation to keep my spaces clean and organized, so here is my "go-to" motivational story.

My husband and I have a dear friend who works at the World Bank. In order to strengthen local economies in developing parts of Africa, he must accurately assess whether or not a local economy is stable enough to make judicious use of new resources (money, supply chains, new technology, and so forth).

I once asked my friend how he could go into a region where he does not speak the language, know the customs, or have any direct access to financial information and make an assessment of economic stability. His answer was so very surprising that I have never forgotten it.

One of several gauges of economic stability my friend uses when he arrives in a new place is a visit to the open markets. He looks to see if the majority of the market's vendors have taken care to organize their produce. If they have stacked their fruit instead of leaving it in messy heaps, if they have swept up and tidied their space, if they have added even a touch of beauty—these are signs that the local economy is more stable than not. How amazingly simple and motivating is that?

Even if they are not World Bank detectives assigned to Africa, people can and do gauge our peacefulness— our emotional and spiritual stability—by observing the care we take with our space. Therefore, if we want to improve our odds of living in emotional and spiritual stability, one thing we can do is mindfully set a peaceful stage by keeping things organized, clean, and beautiful.

Of course, it's not that outward disorganization is equal to inner instability. But, as my World Bank friend observes, the odds of inner stability are higher among those who value outward organization, cleanliness, and beauty. His observations are exactly the motivation I need to get off the couch and clean my house!

Lord Jesus, you are my peace. As I pursue emotional and spiritual peace, Lord, give me the motivation to keep my environment organized, clean, and beautiful.

God Works for Our Good

Popular sayings like "Everything happens for the best" or "Everything happens for a reason" have never really sat well with me. They sound scriptural, or at least as if they were said by some wise and ancient person. But are they?

I think what most people are trying to express when they use such sayings is this incredibly hope-filled truth written in the Scriptures: "And we know that in all things God works for the good of those who love him, who have been called according to his purpose" (Romans 8:28, NIV). The popular sayings and this Scripture passage sound similar enough on the surface, but upon deeper inspection, their meanings are actually entirely different.

Such popular sayings encourage us to think that if we just look at bad things from a different angle or throw a soft-focus lens on them, then we won't ever have to come to terms with how bad they really are. In some way, these sayings spiritualize denial. But denial is never a truly Christian approach to life, and it does not bring us peace.

In the Christian worldview, renaming or denying what is bad can never make it good, palatable, useful, or anything other than bad. Everything that happens is not always for the best. However, by God's power and mercy, the good is possible and should be expected after, in spite of, or right at the same time as the bad. Because of Christ's life, death, and resurrection, the bad can be redeemed. That is the heart of the entire salvation story and something that everyone who has experienced bad things in their lives desperately needs to hear in order to maintain hope for the future.

The truth that God will be working for my good no matter what happens in this life has quieted my soul and given me peace time and time again. It's a Bible verse well worth memorizing.

Lord Jesus, you are my peace. Help me to remember and trust in your words of truth: "And we know that in all things God works for the good of those who love him, who have been called according to his purpose".

Our Relationship with Money

Have you ever thought about the idea that each of us has a relationship with money? That there is more going on between you and me and our green stuff than just numbers? I find the idea fascinating and very helpful in learning how to work with my husband in a more peaceable manner when it comes to making unified financial decisions.

Once after a heated argument about an impending financial decision, my husband said he understood our differences lay not in our priorities but with the fact that I was a "splitter" and he was a "lumper." It was a "eureka" moment for me.

I have a cautious and calculating money personality. I feel at peace and financially secure when I know what our income is and can divvy it up into specific categories. My husband has a casual and companionable money personality. He is at peace and feels financially secure after comparing our general income to our general expenses and seeing that, by and large, the two match up. There are advantages and disadvantages to both personalities, but sparks can fly when we try to make joint decisions. His big-picture generalizations make me feel insecure, and my close accounting makes him feel controlled.

According to Christian financial expert Dave Ramsey, "How we handle money in our relationships involves power, priorities, dreams, passions, and ultimately, our value system. Agreeing on money unlocks so many doors to a strong marriage because money is rarely just about money."[6]

Perhaps you have only ever thought of money as being just about facts and figures. However, reading Ramsey's books or enrolling in a class with his Financial Peace University will expand your understanding about money and give you greater peace in your life. Learning to identify and respect the emotions wrapped up in our different approaches to money hasn't changed my or my husband's individual relationship to money. But it has helped us get and stay on the same page when it comes to making decisions about how we use it.

Lord Jesus, you are my peace. Give me insight into my own relationship with money so that I may enjoy more respectful and more peaceful relationships in my life.

Perfection, with God's Grace

Here is one of the more intimidating passages in the Bible: "You therefore must be perfect, as your heavenly Father is perfect" (Matthew 5:48). Since I know that being perfect is impossible, I have often wondered, "So why does Jesus even ask us to try?"

But then I came up with this analogy for why and how perfection is not only possible but is also meant to be an instrument of great peace in our lives.

If I imagine my life to be like a flower vase, then my goal is not just to fill my vase but to fill it completely (perfectly). But with what can I fill my vase? Well, if I imagine that rocks, marbles, or sand represents my God-given gifts and talents—including works of mercy, praying, and praising God—then I can fill my vase (my life) with them.

The problem, however, is that even the finest-grained sand will have air pockets and won't fill the flower vase perfectly, just as my finest attempts at holiness will always be lacking. However, along comes God, who offers to pour his water into my vase (his grace into my life) and so fills in even the tiniest gaps (my shortcomings) perfectly!

This is how it is possible that when we are filled with God's grace, we are made perfect—no matter how big or small the number or the extent of our acts of holiness, no matter whether we think that what we can contribute to the world is so little in comparison with the saints.

Jesus is not setting us up for failure by commanding us to be perfect. He is setting us up to know peace by knowing what to do the very moment in which the impossibility of perfection dawns on us. In that moment, we are to look to the One who is "the founder and perfecter of our faith" (Hebrews 12:2) and invite him to make up what is lacking in us.

Lord Jesus, you are my peace. Help me seek perfection in you, with you, and through you alone.

Combating House Envy

As I stepped out of the hot summer sun, over the granite threshold, and into the air-conditioned cavernous entryway of my friend's new house, I was seized with "house envy." Of course I was happy that my friend had just moved into this grandiose six-bedroom mansion, complete with a pool that sparkled like a jewel in the exquisitely landscaped yard. Of course I was. But I was also turning six shades of jealous.

So universal is the temptation to desire another person's house that it is specifically listed in the Ten Commandments as one of the things we are told not to covet: "You shall not covet your neighbor's house; you shall not covet your neighbor's wife, or his male servant, or his female servant, or his ox, or his donkey, or anything that is your neighbor's" (Exodus 20:17).

Think about that for a minute. We have already been told not to steal our neighbors' stuff in the seventh commandment, right? Why, then, would God "waste" another commandment to tell us not to even want something belonging to our neighbor? Who cares what we desire, if we actually do the right thing? God cares, that's who, because God is concerned with our attitudes as well as our actions. He knows that long before it might lead us to actually steal from a friend, coveting her stuff will eat away at the peace and gratitude we have for what he has given us and at the love we share with that friend.

I have found that the fastest way to recover from covetousness of any kind is to simply own up to my feelings immediately and to pray just as immediately for the grace to be happy for how God has blessed that person. Standing in my friend's very cool entryway, I said, "Oh my goodness, I am so jealous. How awesome is this place!" To which my good friend replied, "I know! Can you even believe I get to live here? You have to come over and enjoy it with me every day." And just like that, peace was restored in my heart and in our friendship.

Lord Jesus, you are my peace. Help me not to covet what you have given others but to be truly happy for how you have blessed them.

Replacing Bad Attitudes with Virtuous Ones

When we are seeking to meet everyday challenges with more peaceful hearts, the attitudes we carry with us are vitally important. So then why is it so hard to eliminate bad attitudes?

Jesus told the story of the seven unclean spirits returning to the house with the one who had left (Matthew 12:43-45). But if the man in that story had invited even one virtuous attitude into his house, the sign on his heart would have read, "No Vacancy." If we truly want more peace in our lives, it will not be enough for us to merely eliminate bad attitudes; we must replace them with virtuous ones. I created the following prayer using the list of heavenly virtues found in James 3:16-17 and 1 Corinthians 13:4-13:

Give me the grace, Lord,
To be pure of intentions,
To love peace,
To be considerate,
To be submissive to you,
To be full of mercy
To be impartial,

To be sincere,
To be patient,
To be kind,
To rejoice in the truth,
To bear all things,
To believe all things,
To hope all things,
To endure all things,
To abide in love.

Which of these will you invite into your heart today?

Lord Jesus, you are my peace. As I seek to be more peaceful, help me to not only sweep away bad attitudes from my heart, but also to invite virtuous ones in.

Creative Organization

Does anyone else remember mitten clips? They have saved my sanity on countless occasions, especially when trying to get everyone out the door on time to church or school on snowy winter mornings. I love mitten clips so much, in fact, that a few years ago I adapted the idea to my own winter wardrobe.

One particularly hectic winter, I kept misplacing one or both of my mittens, and it drove me crazy! Every time we needed to go somewhere, I found myself anxiously digging through piles of hats and scarves and boots, desperately trying to locate them. Even after I did find them, my anxiety level was so amped up that my peace of mind was nowhere to be found.

Clearly I needed a new approach to the problem, but unlike the kids, I had more than one coat (plus I thought a grown woman using mitten clips was really just a bit too much!). However, keeping the idea in mind, I went to a winter clearance sale and bought five pairs of the exact same medium-weight mittens. I stuck one pair in the pockets of each of my jackets, essentially copying the idea of mitten clips but for multiple jackets. Now, for a small price, I no longer have to even think about mittens before leaving the house. If I have a jacket, I have mittens. Every winter since then, I have been a much less anxious, much nicer mommy.

Sometimes restoring peace of mind is as easy as identifying what is robbing us of peace and rethinking our approach to it. Since adapting the idea of mitten clips to my own winter wardrobe, I have applied the same principle in other ways, and it really reduces my anxiety. For example, I have established one place in the house for all cell-phone chargers, one place next to the TV for all remotes, and I keep the family van stocked with water bottles rather than trying to remember to grab them on the way out the door.

Ah, mitten clips—what a great invention!

Lord Jesus, you are my peace. Help me to recognize and creatively organize anything in my life that is causing a disproportionate amount of anxiety.

Showing Appreciation

My husband's job entails a fair amount of travel. Thankfully, he is rarely away on weekends, but his irregular trips during the week can still be difficult. Throw in a night or two of his getting home late or of me trying to get to my volunteer commitments after dinner, and all of a sudden I begin to feel like a single parent.

If his work schedule were more predictable, I would have backup plans, babysitters on tap, and a broader understanding from family and friends about the times I cannot follow through on reasonably made plans. As it is, however—and even though I know that sporadic travel is just a part of my husband's job—the erratic doubling of my workload and adjusting of responsibilities can leave me feeling unappreciated and resentful.

Are there areas of hardship in your life that are practically invisible to those around you? Are you caring for elderly parents on top of raising a family? Are you regularly supervising more teenagers than just your own after school and on weekends? There can be many unseen or sporadic strains in life, and we can often feel resentful when no one seems to acknowledge them or thank us for what we do.

Pope Francis has suggested three phrases that all families should use in order to live in harmony. "If families can say these three things, they will be fine. 'Sorry,' 'excuse me,' 'thank you.' How often do we say 'thank you' in our families? How often do we say 'thank you' to those who help us, those close to us, those at our side throughout life? All too often we take everything for granted!"[7]

In truth, intermittent work travel is as difficult for my husband as it is for me, just for different reasons. But if I were to take Pope Francis' advice, I would look for opportunities to thank my husband for providing for our family instead of harboring resentment over his unavoidable absences. Simply showing appreciation for what the other person is doing can go a long way toward helping us bear up under hardships and not feel taken for granted.

Lord Jesus, you are my peace. Help me to acknowledge hardships and not take other people for granted.

God Alone Is Enough

Let nothing upset you, let nothing startle you.
All things pass; God does not change.
Patience wins all it seeks.
Whoever has God lacks nothing:
God alone is enough.

What is holding us back from living as St. Teresa of Avila advises in her famous "bookmark" prayer?[8]

At this point in my life, I know worry holds me back. Sometimes I stop myself in the middle of praying because I realize that the thread of my prayers has changed into a knotted string of worries. The weight of my responsibilities holds me back too, especially when there are so many people depending on my husband and me (but then that's just anxiety tying my stomach in knots again!).

Yet what if you and I were to begin to live as if God alone were enough? What would the practical implications be? On our short list would surely be our ability to be more peaceful with the people in our lives. We would be more forgiving because we would be so aware of God's mercy in our own life. We would not be as needy because God's love would be enough for us. We would know that in his eyes, we are truly worthy, beautiful, valuable, and capable, and that what we do or how much we have is not who we are. We would be more generous, even in tough times, and misfortunes would not disturb our trust in God.

If we were to live as if God alone were enough, we would tend to all our earthly responsibilities faithfully and yet hold them loosely. Our sense of well-being and security would be stable, and the peace and goodness of that stability would overflow into all our other relationships and into all our responsibilities.

Lord Jesus, you are my peace. Help me to know that you alone are enough.

The Trap of Minimalism

When I was younger in my journey of faith, I didn't understand all the fuss about things like going to daily Mass or getting to Confession more than once a year, much less praying the Rosary or a novena. If they weren't required by the Church, I thought, then why do them? I'm afraid many of us fall into the trap of minimalism in living out our faith, maybe because we are used to taking the minimalist approach in other areas of our lives as well.

For example, I treasure meals when our whole family can all sit down together and enjoy delicious food. But grocery shopping can be so time-consuming. Therefore, it's not uncommon for me to think, "What is the minimum I need to pick up at the grocery store this week?" So I'll buy milk, eggs, bread, fruit, cold cereal, potatoes, cheese, coffee or creamer, and maybe a bag of chips.

But let me invite you to examine that list and ask yourself this: what can this woman possibly make for a sit-down meal with only those ingredients? The truth is, very little. If my goal in shopping and feeding my family were only to keep us from starving, minimalism might be good enough. My goal, however, is actually even bigger and loftier than enjoying a great meal. My goal is to capitalize on our common need for physical sustenance to nourish and strengthen us spiritually and emotionally. So minimalist shopping simply doesn't cut it.

Which brings me back to daily Mass. If I want merely to fulfill the technical requirements of the Church, I could attend the shortest possible Mass every weekend and likewise participate in the life of the Church only as required. But would this minimalist approach bring me the deepest possible joy, show me how to persevere under trial, or give me the strength to love, forgive, and live in peace? Not likely. In giving us the manifold gifts of Scripture and tradition, God shows that he has bigger and loftier goals for us than just keeping us from spiritual starvation. In these gifts the Lord desires to nourish and strengthen us, and so he invites us to load up our plates.

Lord Jesus, you are my peace. Protect me from spiritual minimalism so that I may be strengthened by the spiritual banquet you have set before me.

Reducing the Clutter

When we moved from a small apartment to a bigger house, I had a hard time understanding why it seemed as if our living space was more cluttered, not less. After all, our family size had not increased. Eventually, I realized that the problem was with the increase in the amount of things we had purchased and were using.

When, for example, we hosted a large dinner party at our new house, I went to a thrift store and picked up a second set of dishes. After the party, I simply put the new dishes in the cupboard behind the old ones. I didn't intend on using them on a daily basis, just keeping them on hand for future parties.

Unfortunately, it turns out that when you are rushed to get dinner on the table, it takes a lot more discipline to clean and reuse one set of currently dirty dishes than it does to just grab dishes from a second set of clean ones sitting there on the shelf. So what began to happen regularly was that instead of having one set of dirty dishes cluttering up the counter, now I had two!

It's true that even if you have less stuff for the same number of people, the amount of cleaning that needs to be done remains the same. The potential for clutter, however, is far less, because stuff is what causes clutter, not how often it needs to be cleaned. This math works for bath towels and clothing as well as for dishes, by the way.

The solution to reducing clutter and reclaiming my peace of mind was not to move back into an apartment. What I did was take the extra dishes out of the kitchen cupboards and store them somewhere else. And after assigning one towel to each person, I also hid all the new guest towels. How to restore a cluttered house to order? Use the same stuff more often.

Lord Jesus, you are my peace. Help me to examine the amount of clutter in my home and consider reducing the amount of things I use on a regular basis.

Speaking Up or Staying Silent?

Sometimes we take the phrase "speaking the truth in love" as permission to say whatever we feel like saying as long as we say it in a loving way. This approach doesn't leave room for the possibility that sometimes the most loving thing to do is to say nothing.

Knowing when and how to say something certainly requires unceasing prayer, especially in times of disagreement or heated conflict. Knowing when to zip our lips, however, also requires unceasing prayer and, more important, the realization that sometimes silence is even more powerful than words, even if they are sincerely intended and spoken in a loving way.

So when do we speak up and when do we stay quiet?

If we look at the origin of the phrase "speaking the truth in love," it is actually part of a longer discourse by St. Paul in which he is specifically talking about unity in the body of Christ:

> May [we] no longer be children, tossed to and fro by the waves and carried about by every wind of doctrine, by human cunning, by craftiness in deceitful schemes. Rather, speaking the

truth in love, we are to grow up in every way into him who is the head, into Christ, from whom the whole body, joined and held together by every joint with which it is equipped, when each part is working properly, makes the body grow so that it builds itself up in love. (Ephesians 4:14-16)

Whether the "whole body" that St. Paul talks about is an entire community of people or my spouse and I, the goal of maturing in our communal faith is to be able to live in a state of unity, steadiness, and peace that is anchored in Christ. So we can ask ourselves, "Will what I want to say contribute to the building up of the whole body, or will it simply let everyone know that I am, yet again, right? Will what I want to say put the 'Great Me' on an even higher pedestal, or will it strengthen those around me to choose the way of Christ, which is the way of peace?"

Lord Jesus, you are my peace. Guide me in knowing when to speak up and when to keep silent for the sake of building up true peace.

The Peal of Church Bells

Has every kid's sports team in the country now decided that it's okay for games to be scheduled on Sunday mornings? And that if your kid misses the game, he's thrown off the team? This really chafes at my peacefulness.

Technically, we can go to church on Saturday evenings, and we often do, but it just feels as if the tail is chasing the dog when we are constantly being asked to "work in" church around sports instead of the other way around. For some families, this tension is felt with other activities like theatre or band practice. But for all, the experience of the Sabbath can be reduced to a rushed "getting to" Mass instead of what God meant it to be: a generous invitation to rest and be refreshed (*Catechism of the Catholic Church*, 2172).

I have talked with other Christian parents about this tension. Opinions on how to handle commitments on Sundays are as varied as the families themselves. I have also searched through Scripture and have found this guiding proverb in the Book of James: "But above all, my brothers, do not swear, either by heaven or by earth or by any other oath, but let your 'yes' be yes and your 'no' be no, so that you may not fall under condemnation" (5:12).

Letting our "yes be yes" and our "no be no" works on so many dimensions to give us peace in our lives but especially with our schedules. When we commit to something, we keep our word. That means letting our yes be yes, but it also means letting our no be no, because whether we choose to do something or choose not to do it, we keep our word, accept the consequences, and do not let others make us feel guilty.

Whether it is with sports teams or other organized pastimes, we sometimes feel trapped into Sunday morning participation, but we really are not. We can sit down in advance and choose our family's level of participation prayerfully and carefully, and then communicate it to those in charge. The blare of the coach's or any other bullhorn does not have to completely drown out the peal of the church bells.

Lord Jesus, you are my peace. Open my ears to hear and heed your call to celebrate the Sabbath.

Clothe Yourself in Joy

Time for a quick reality check. Do you wake up to joy? Do you wake up expecting a brilliant, peace-filled day with the Lord? If yes, way to go! If not, then today is the day to turn the page and start the all-new habit of clothing yourself in joy, because joy gives birth to peace.

The psalmist tells us, "Wait for the Lord; / be strong, and let your heart take courage; / wait for the LORD!" (27:14). In other words, don't just put on that same old backpack of worries and trudge out the door again today. Empty it at the foot of the cross and don't look back! Believe that today a breakthrough may come. Believe that no matter what may happen, Jesus is alive and is going to be with you through it all (Matthew 28:20).

Conventional wisdom says that it takes approximately one month to break an old habit and replace it with a new one. So commit yourself to waking up to joy and clothing yourself with peace for the next four weeks. Find a little song of praise to the Lord and sing it as soon as you hop out of bed. Learn a little prayer of surrender and recite it each morning as you head to the coffeemaker. Discover the joy of thanking God in advance for the good he will be working in you today.

In doing these things, you will be choosing to put on the qualities of Christ as if they were as real and tangible as the clothing you also choose to wear—because they are! Listen to what St. Paul has to tell us about being clothed in Christ:

> *Put on* then, as God's chosen ones, holy and beloved, compassionate hearts, kindness, humility, meekness, and patience, bearing with one another. . . . And above all these *put on* love, which binds everything together in perfect harmony. And let the peace of Christ rule in your hearts. . . . And be thankful. (Colossians 3:12-15, emphasis added)

Lord Jesus, you are my peace. Help me to clothe myself in you so that your peace might rule in my heart.

Creating a Prayer Corner

Do you ever visit enormous furniture showrooms just for fun? I do! Wandering around stores like IKEA sparks my imagination in the same way that visiting Disneyland does for young children—only it's a lot less expensive. (That is, provided you don't actually buy anything at the furniture showroom!)

What would it feel like to have those bright purple throw pillows in my living room or that wall-sized piece of art dominating my bedroom? Something intrigues me about the mindful use and arrangement of objects and colors to create atmosphere.

It also reminds me of one of the best tips I ever received as a newlywed: to set the stage for daily communion with God by establishing a prayer corner in our home. Over the past twenty-five years of marriage and family life, having a prayer corner has not only visibly shown our openness to God's presence in our home, but it has also helped to create an atmosphere of peace.

A prayer corner does not have to be elaborate, but it should be aesthetically pleasing and inviting. (This is where a field trip to a furniture showroom comes in.) Elements to consider would be a comfortable place to sit, good lighting, and an organized place to keep items like a Bible, a rosary, or the *Catechism*. A crucifix or other artistic reminders of the faith could also help to create a peaceful, contemplative atmosphere. You might want to keep a notebook and pencil handy to write down Scripture verses, thoughts, or inspirations from the Lord, and maybe even add an iPod dock or CD player to play uplifting music.

Over the years, having a prayer corner in our home has helped me to actually get to praying instead of wasting precious time hunting for my Bible or rosary. Another peaceable bonus? When I'm in my corner, the rest of the family knows not to interrupt me!

If you are not able to visit a furniture showroom, consider viewing one online or treating yourself to a home-decorating magazine. Use the inspiration to create and enjoy your own prayer corner.

Lord Jesus, you are my peace. Inspire me and show me how to welcome you into my home with a prayer corner.

Shalom

Shalom is a Hebrew word meaning "peace." It is used both as a greeting and a farewell, but its full meaning transcends its common usage. To wish someone "Shalom" is to say that you want that person to know contentment, completeness, well-being, and tranquility. "Shalom" in this deepest, richest sense is a gift that Jesus is forever offering us.

Jesus offered his twelve apostles shalom when he was telling them about his impending death and resurrection: "Peace I leave with you; my peace I give to you. Not as the world gives do I give to you. Let not your hearts be troubled, neither let them be afraid" (John 14:27). Yet why would Jesus offer his apostles contentment, completeness, and tranquility in the face of what he knew they would have to endure between then and when they would see him again after his resurrection? Shouldn't he have offered them courage or, better yet, an escape plan instead of peace?

No. Jesus offered them peace because shalom was the gift of God that would sustain them through the upcoming ordeal and, indeed, through their entire lives once he had returned to the Father in heaven.

Do we sometimes ask Jesus for an escape plan instead of accepting the shalom he is forever offering us? I know I do! To open my heart and accept Jesus' gift of shalom takes a tremendous amount of trust, which I do not always have. Neither did the apostles at times. Unable to trust Jesus with his bodily safety, Peter rejected Jesus' shalom by denying that he even knew Jesus (John 18:17, 25, 27). Unable to trust others' accounts of Jesus' resurrection, Thomas rejected Jesus' shalom by refusing to believe that Jesus had risen until he saw him with his own eyes (20:24-28).

And yet we know that Jesus never rescinds his offer of deep and abiding peace. After his resurrection, Jesus' first words to his apostles were "Peace be with you" (John 20:19). Whether we have failed to accept Jesus' shalom only once or hundreds of times, Jesus offers it again and again. He wants each of us to know the contentment and completeness that only he can bring us. This time, will you open your heart and accept it?

Lord Jesus, you are my peace. Open my heart to your shalom.

Finding Peace through Friendship

Very often I assume that no one else has to endure the little "pinpricks" that I do: the ingratitude of my children, the presumption of my colleagues, and the demands of my extended family. In the big picture of life, these nuisances are mere paper cuts. So why do they have the power to rob me of so much peace? Why do I struggle to maintain a regularly joyful attitude and to remember the goodness of my life?

When I find myself asking these sorts of unanswerable questions—whether they are about legitimate life crises or small aggravations—a conversation with a good and godly friend is often what I need to correct my outlook and restore my peace. My youngest son's godmother, Karen, is one such friend. Not only does Karen listen to and laugh with me over my little tales of woe, but she also has the knack of pointing me to an even bigger pool of friends: the saints.

"I always find peace and perspective in reading about the lives of the saints, especially St. Thérèse of Lisieux," Karen shared with me once when we were talking about coping with little annoyances. "She shows us the kind of peace that comes with acceptance, especially of the small things that can get under your skin."

When she was starting a Catholic kids' club, Karen introduced me to St. John Bosco, the patron saint of boys and youth. Remembering St. John Bosco's always holy but also very human approach to working with young people has restored my peace of mind many times, whether it was while parenting my own boys or while working at a local Catholic elementary school.

I am blessed to have a small group of close women friends here on earth and an even larger suite of friends up in heaven. By the model of their lives, by their prayers, and because they keep pointing me back to Jesus, they have all helped me endure life's big injuries as well as the little pinpricks. Godly friendships remind us of the big picture of life and help us to hang on to the peace that Jesus offers through every little thing.

Lord Jesus, you are my peace. Open my heart to good and godly friends and to the friendship of the saints.

Joy, Not Defensiveness

By most historical and cultural frames of reference, to live a fully Christian life is to be countercultural, and to be countercultural is not always peaceful. Jesus experienced this firsthand, of course, and warned us, "If the world hates you, know that it has hated me before it hated you"(John 15:18).

My friend Amy shared how she has come to have peace even when others react negatively to her family of ten children.

"When our small family turned medium, and then our medium family turned large, I spent years in an angry, defensive mode. I got angry when people accused me of 'ruining the environment,' especially since we recycle everything, use cloth diapers, and wear hand-me-down clothing almost exclusively.

"My prayer to God for many years was to find peace in our decision to live providentially and to not feel persecuted for what we have freely chosen to do. Through prayer I realized that how we were living was unusual, and in some ways it was meant to be an uncomfortable witness to life. I needed to realize that we are all called to spread the gospel but that everyone is called to do it in a different way.

"Instead of being defensive when people asked about our family, I had to learn to answer in a way that would be pleasing to God. If I answered nosy questions (which often felt like persecutions) in a nasty way, then people would shrug me off and assume that I was miserable because I had so many kids. I also eventually learned not to focus on people that do not understand but on those who love us as we are."

Remembering that Jesus is the final victor can help us have joy instead of being defensive about living differently than others. "I have said these things to you, that in me you may have peace," Jesus promised. "In the world you will have tribulation. But take heart; I have overcome the world" (John 16:33).

Lord Jesus, you are my peace. Instead of succumbing to defensiveness, help me to embrace you and my faith with love and joy.

Focusing on the Beauty

My oldest son attends law school in our town. A couple of weeks into his first semester, he gave me a tour of the school. The ivy-covered Gothic-style buildings and manicured spaces were so inspiring that I felt as if I had been transported in space and time to the set of some epic movie. As my son escorted me through carved granite doorways and past ancient wooden tables, I pulled out a small camera and started snapping away as if I were on a tour of Rome.

The interesting thing is that the law school is located smack in the middle of a busy city. Modern art sculptures populate the green space around the buildings and some fairly grimy fraternity houses are packed in along the back streets, creating a stark architectural contrast. When taking pictures, however, I could use my camera lens to select the beauty that I wanted to capture and crop out the less pleasing images that I did not.

I am quite familiar with using my camera to self-select the world I want to see and record on film. But while photographing my son's campus, it occurred to me that I could apply the power of self-selection to other areas of my life as well.

Why do I allow the clutter in my house to grab my attention more than the areas that are picked up? Why do I allow the things that are in need of repair bother me more than allowing the things that are not broken to give me reason to give thanks?

Recently, I have challenged myself to find something to be grateful for before going to the Lord with a request for help. "Thank you, Lord, that the washing machine is working," I might pray when I look at the gridlocked calendar. "Thank you, Lord, that I had a good laugh with my teenager this morning," I might pray when I need to balance the budget later in the day. Beginning my prayers with self-selecting gratitude lowers my stress level and gives me an incredible amount of internal peace.

Lord Jesus, you are my peace. Help me to focus my attention on whatever things are beautiful and inspiring around me. If anything is excellent or praiseworthy, help me to be grateful for these things (Philippians 4:8).

First Things First

I have a friend, Deanna, who shares that in order to walk peaceably through her day, she gets up before the sun to pray. Of course, she is imitating our Lord in doing this: "And rising very early in the morning, while it was still dark, he departed and went out to a desolate place, and there he prayed" (Mark 1:35).

I must confess that while I have experienced the incredible power of early-morning prayer, I have also found it quite challenging. It seems as if I am forever in need of just a little more sleep. Even when I try to get up a mere fifteen minutes earlier, the result is often more time spent pushing the snooze button on my alarm clock than praying even a single decade of my rosary beads. I'm pretty sure that God has a good laugh on the mornings when I actually do wake up with the alarm clock and grab my rosary beads but then stay in bed and attempt to pray. Those are some of my most self-deluded attempts at multitasking, for sure!

But here's the reason I keep renewing my attempts to pray first thing in the morning: prayer is how Jesus showed us to live by the grace of God, no matter what happens between sun up and sun down.

The truth is that so many of our days pass as we had expected they would—a bit of this, a bit of that, some hard work, some good times. But then along comes a challenging day, and life is thrown into rough and uncharted waters.

Deanna experienced this a few years ago when, out of the blue, she had two strokelike episodes. To this day, doctors have not been able to tell Deanna exactly what happened. But it was beautiful to watch how peacefully she walked with the Lord even on the toughest days of her recovery. I know it was her commitment to early-morning prayer that allowed Deanna to surrender her fears and have peace.

Jesus' example in Scripture and Deanna's story remind me that prayer paves the way for peaceful living. Which is why it's best to get to it first thing in the morning!

Lord Jesus, you are my peace. Wake me up to your love and grace each morning so that I may know your peace.

Sustained by God's Faithfulness

Nine times out of ten, when I ask other women to tell me about a time when they have felt God's peace, a beautiful story unfolds about how they have experienced God presence, providence, and protection during challenging times. My friend Lisa shares how God's presence during a difficult pregnancy sustained her faith for many years.

"My first two pregnancies had ended in miscarriages, and because I had been born with a severe birth defect in my abdomen, I began to believe that I might not be able to carry a child to term.

"On one particular evening, I was alone, straightening up our apartment and humming to myself. I had been playing the viola in some performances of the *Messiah*, and I began paying attention to the text from Isaiah that accompanies the aria I was humming, 'He shall feed his flock like a shepherd. . . .' When I got to '. . . and gently lead those that are with young,' I suddenly knew with absolute certainty that this was God answering my prayer! I knew that everything was going to be okay. I had no worries about the tiny life inside me or of my ability to physically carry the baby to term.

"This was God's peace washing over me, along with a healthy dose of elation! I cried in gratitude for being gifted with such assuredness. Believe me, that aria was pretty much the theme song for my entire pregnancy— which ended blessedly with the birth of my daughter, Maria.

"Now, many years and two sons later, when my faith wavers, it is experiences like this one that keep me going and bring me back to belief. Very often it is through the words of a hymn that I sense God's presence and hear him speaking to me. I confess that it is in my darkest moments that he is able to reach me best. But as my relationship with him continues and deepens, I am better able to sense him reaching out to me, offering his peace and his protection, in my everyday life."

Lord Jesus, you are my peace. Remind me of your faithfulness when my faith wavers.

Gentleness, Wisdom, Love

Have you ever dreaded getting together with extended family or neighbors because you just don't have the energy for the arguments that may crop up? I have! However, as I've matured, I've figured out that having a biblical response to argumentative people can make all the difference.

When someone attacks our beliefs, or us, our natural reaction can be to launch an immediate counterattack. This approach rarely ever brings peace to a relationship. Our counterargument, no matter how true, more often results in a flare-up of tempers rather than in helping us simmer down and resolve the issue.

A passage from the Book of Proverbs shows us how to respond to people who may be looking to start an argument: "A soft answer turns away wrath, / but a harsh word stirs up anger" (15:1). By making gentleness and empathy our first response, we can often defuse the destructive power of an emotionally charged situation before it results in an explosive confrontation.

Then, once we have defused the conflict "time bomb," the next verse in Proverbs shows us how, through the power of the Holy Spirit, we may actually be able to dismantle it: "The tongue of the wise commends knowledge" (15:2). Unfortunately, a wise tongue alone may still not make our knowledge acceptable to others, no matter what the strength or logic of our argument is.

There are two big mistakes we can make in facing conflict: to think that we can hop over the initial step of defusing emotions and go straight to the dismantling of ideas or, even more foolish, to think that we can do either the defusing or the dismantling with our own cleverness instead of with God's grace.

Whether it's around the dinner table at a family Thanksgiving or the picnic table at a neighborhood barbeque, with God's grace we can defuse emotional time bombs with gentleness. Then we may even be able to move someone towards the truth with the wisdom that God gives us. Our greatest witness to peace, however, may lie in loving others, no matter how difficult they are.

Lord Jesus, you are my peace. Grant me grace to treat argumentative people with gentleness, wisdom, and love.

Focus and Trust

There are few areas in life that cause us more angst than finances. Fortunately, Jesus' financial advice is so very simple and universal: "For where your treasure is, there your heart will be also" (Matthew 6:21). From this verse, and from the entire sixth chapter of the Gospel of Matthew, we learn that Jesus wants us to calmly and quietly focus on the kingdom of heaven and to have childlike trust that God knows what things we do and do not need to get there.

The more closely aligned our focus and our trust, the more peace we will have in making financial decisions of all kinds. The story of the rich young man shows us what can happen when our focus and trust are not aligned.

And as he was setting out on his journey, a man ran up and knelt before him and asked him, "Good Teacher, what must I do to inherit eternal life?" And Jesus said to him, "Why do you call me good? No one is good except God alone. You know the commandments: 'Do not murder, Do not commit adultery, Do not steal, Do not bear false witness, Do not defraud, Honor your father and mother.'" And he said to him, "Teacher, all these I have kept from my youth." And Jesus, looking at him, loved him, and said to him, "You lack one thing: go, sell all that you have and give to the poor, and you will have treasure in heaven; and come, follow me." Disheartened by the saying, he went away sorrowful, for he had great possessions. (Mark 10:17-22)

The rich young man was focused, but he could not trust Jesus enough to obey him, and so he went away without peace. In which area do you need to grow in order to have your earthly life better aligned with eternal life, in your focus on God or in your trust of him? Whichever it is (and maybe it's both!), know for certain that God looks at you with love and that everything he asks of you is for your good.

Lord Jesus, you are my peace. Guide me to focus on the kingdom of heaven and to trust in you for all my earthly needs.

Stepping Out in Faith

I have a friend who has faced a host of challenges in her life. She is a breast-cancer survivor, she earned her master's degree while raising young children, and she has moved cross-country several times. She also has a spouse who travels extensively. In spite of these challenges, this woman is a model of peaceful living.

And yet she hesitates to share the secret of her peace because she is currently going through a difficult time with an emotionally fragile teenager. Her faith in Christ is giving her personal peace in the midst of this trial, as it has during her other trials. But the uncertainty of the outcome of her child's situation has eroded her confidence in sharing her faith publicly. I completely understand my friend's hesitancy, but at the same time, I am sad for her.

Sometimes we do not share our faith in Christ with others because we feel as if our imperfections, trials, or doubts disqualify us from talking about the things of God. But God did not say that all our troubles had to be resolved before we could be witnesses of his love. It is not hypocritical to speak of his love and mercy even when our lives are not perfect. Rather, it is human.

By his mercy, God may not quiet our storms, but he does offer us peace in the midst of them. He wants us to have his peace for our own sake, but he may also ask us to publicly step out in faith and share the source of our peace for the benefit of others. Jesus may not invite us to literally step out of a boat in the middle of a storm, as he did with Peter on the Sea of Galilee (Matthew 14:25-29). But he does invite us to step out in faith and live in a way that causes other people to wonder why we are so peaceful in the midst of life's storms.

Lord Jesus, you are my peace. Thank you for calling me out of the boat in order to be a witness to the power of your peace and protection.

Trusting in God's Providence

Unemployment and moving are at the top of the list of stressful experiences. One friend, Linda, shares what she has learned about God's peace when facing both at once.

"We found out that my husband's employment situation was about to drastically change. At the time, we had six of our eight children still living at home, plus two elderly family members. We started to pray.

"I was scared but open to wherever God would lead us, whether that meant my husband's staying in his present job and taking on a second job or all of us moving to a different state if necessary. Being open to a move was difficult because we loved our life in the small town where my husband had grown up. We had built our dream home, had all our family and friends nearby, and enjoyed our parish. But after twenty-five years of marriage, we were committed to doing whatever was necessary to stay together as a family. Eventually, the call came for a job in a different state.

"Selling our home was not easy. The financial concerns were mounting as my husband left to start his new job, bringing one of our high school-aged daughters with him. I stayed back to try to sell the house. For six long months, it was a very stressful time for all of us, until we finally decided to reunite and join my husband and daughter and leave the sale of the house to God's providence. After much prayer, the house finally did sell.

"Coming to this new town has been filled with unexpected blessings. The faith community here is like nothing we've ever experienced elsewhere. I know we have a better chance than ever before of nurturing a life of grace for all of us.

"I spent my whole life fighting and struggling to keep my faith alive. It was hard, but now it's time for me to be fed, and it could never have happened without the blessings of looming unemployment and the need to move."

Lord Jesus, you are my peace. When I am stressed and scared, help me to trust in your providence.

The Father's Good Pleasure

My friend Jen shares a lesson that she learned during her time as a missionary in Tanzania.

"I had always acted as if prayer needed to be filtered. I treated my prayer requests like e-mail, putting them in labels and files. One file might be labeled 'Hopeless,' another 'Too big,' and another 'Pending.'

"I also 'triaged' prayer, sorting through my needs and then choosing prayers that I thought were reasonable, acceptable, or doable. It was as if I were asking for things for Christmas and thinking, 'Well, of all the things I need the most, this is it. So I will ask for this and hold back from these, because it is rude to ask for too much at one time.'

"But Jesus tells us to ask and ask and ask again! Now I've decided to ask for everything. And what's amazing is that I've never in my life had so much peace!

"Part of our finding peace is in knowing that we have an almighty Father in heaven who really does want to give us good things. Jesus said, 'Fear not, little flock, for it is your Father's good pleasure to give you the kingdom' (Luke 12:32). It gives me such peace—knowing that he doesn't want me to fear or worry, knowing that he also cares for me tenderly like a shepherd for his sheep, and knowing that he enjoys giving me good things and the kingdom.

"Jesus doesn't consider it rude or impudent to ask for good things. He says, 'Ask away! Don't worry about being rude or impudent or a pain in the neck. Don't hold anything back. Just ask me. If it is good for you, it is my good pleasure to give it. If it is not good for you and not my will, I'll lovingly tell you no. If it is not the right time, I'll let you know that as well. But trust in me. It is my good pleasure to answer your many requests and to give you what you need.'"

Lord Jesus, you are my peace. Teach me to ask for all that I need and to believe that it is your pleasure to provide it.

Gifts of Encouragement

Thirty years ago, I received a Christmas present that would change my life. It came from my mother, a woman so artistically gifted and creative that each year the wrapping paper and bows on the boxes beneath our Christmas tree would be as splendid as the gifts within them. That Christmas morning it was obvious that my mom had been keeping her artistic eye on my progress in a high school photography class, for when I unwrapped an unusually flat box, I was astonished to find two of my own color photographs enlarged and mounted on museum-quality photo boards.

Seeing enlargements of my own photographs uncovered for me what would become one of the most important passions of my life: photography. My mother's gift to me was not so much the photographs themselves, however, but the encouragement of showing me that I had a creative talent.

Encouragement is a gift that is always appreciated and is never out of season. It is one of the most valuable acts of peace and kindness that we can give to someone.

I have a friend and fellow photographer, Donna, who maintains a blog that is dedicated entirely to the giving of sincere encouragement. It was inspired by this Bible verse: "Make it your ambition to lead a quiet life and attend to your own business and work with your hands" (1 Thessalonians 4:11, NASB).

In the online world of blogging, which can get a bit narcissistic, Donna's blog quietly stands out from the norm, like the creative wrapping on my mom's Christmas presents. She often concludes her entries with simple yet powerful phrases like these: "Add to the beauty." "Love and encourage one another." "Lead a quiet life." "You have value because God values you."[9]

What would happen if we just took one of Donna's phrases—"Add to the beauty"—and tried to live it? How would I do that today? How could you? I can feel my emotions taking a break from commonplace anxiety about all that is wrong with the world and settling on the higher plateau of giving praise to God for all that is good and right.

Lord Jesus, you are my peace. Focus my thoughts on giving encouragement to those around me.

Relying on His Grace

Sometimes life just doesn't work out as we had planned. This fact is not meant to rob us of our peace but to help us learn to rely on God's grace. Justine, remarried and living far away from her extended family, shares this story.

"My husband and I had always agreed that our goal was to move back to New England 'sometime in the future.' The details of when and how this return move would occur had never been quite mapped out.

"During our youngest child's junior year of high school, my husband took a job in New Hampshire and was able to work from our home in Indiana. We hoped that we would move after she graduated and began to set the plan in motion. The job market did not support this plan, and within nine months my husband was looking for work again in Indiana. The disappointment of this 'tease' cost me quite a bit of peace. I had to place this dream back in God's hands for his timing.

"When I find myself anxious and impatient for our move to happen, I look to the fruit of my time here and make a mental list of all the good things that have happened, of the blessings that our children have experienced because of our presence together in this place. I also recognize the many blessings of being at peace with God's timing for where we live: I am able to give more of myself in daily activity, I have become more present to those with whom I live and work, and I have learned to love more deeply than ever before. I have also grown in my faith, from that of a secure, 'protected' child to a more mature adult faith in which I realize that I must trust and rely on God's grace to guide me through the unknowns."

Like Justine, each of us has some way in which life has not gone according to plan. Can we respond as she has, by placing our dreams back in God's hands and relying on his grace to guide us through our unknowns?

Lord Jesus, you are my peace. Help me to trust in and rely on your grace alone.

Peace with Our Body Image

Why do we buy into the fabrication that we are the sum of our dress size? Why do we compulsively offer excuses, to no one in particular, for why we are eating dessert? Without going into all the inaccurate and even toxic cultural expectations of what our bodies should look like, I think it is safe to say that we are living in a time when maintaining a healthy body image taxes most women's sense of personal peace. No body image is safe in a culture that encourages us to compare ourselves to unnaturally thin fashion models and airbrushed photos of celebrities.

I wish I were immune to these toxic comparisons or at least had been able to give my daughters a dose of immunity. Knowing a thought process is toxic, however, and knowing how to not let it poison our psyches are two separate matters. Frankly, I am not immune, but I am not without ideas either.

One technique I have found to restore my peace is to literally wash away the bad messages and images with the positive. Like spraying the inside of a garbage can with a hose, I purge those negative body images by showering them with spiritually healthy thoughts and images.

And what are spiritually healthy thoughts and images? Those that point us toward the truth that we are beautiful in God's eyes and not objects for others' eyes. Magazines, catalogs, or web pages that objectify women (and in many cases, men too) get tossed and replaced with ones that promote the opposite. You might think that's impossible in today's image-saturated world. Difficult, yes, but not impossible, and maintaining peace with my body image is worth the fight.

Another simple and practical technique is to just wear clothes that fit at the moment. If after getting dressed, I can tell that I am going to spend the day tugging at my shirt or feeling pinched at my waistline, I force myself to find a new outfit.

I know I am at peace with my body image when I put more time and energy into feeling healthy and comfortable than in worrying what someone else might think of my appearance.

Lord Jesus, you are my peace. Thank you, Lord, for the body you have given me. Help me to love it as you do.

More than Being Right

Being truthful has a broader meaning than just being right or correct. Truth includes not just objective facts but people too. And being aware of that nuance can give us great peace in our relationships.

For example, when baking cookies, the temperature at which the oven should be set is a fact given in the recipe. If one of my teenagers hopes to speed up the baking time by setting the oven at a higher temperature and then burns the cookies, I would be right in saying, "Setting the temperature that high was wrong! If you had only followed the directions, the smoke detector would have never woken up the baby from her nap!"

But if the same thing happened, a truthful (and graceful) response would sound more like this: "Oh boy, that's a lot of smoke! The oven temperature was way too high, but don't worry, I've made that mistake before too. Go get your sister from her crib, and I'll put the cookie sheet outside."

Did you hear how that worked? What was right about the oven temperature and even about the negative consequences of burned cookies and a screaming baby was not compromised. The truth that my teen was not the only one who had ever tried to hasten a chore by breaking a rule was brought into the situation immediately, however, and it made all the difference. Being truthful accounts for the flawed human beings involved in any situation.

Of course, this is much more difficult when we are talking about politics or the hot-button topics of the day. And yet the same rules apply. We are never just dealing with sets of rights and wrongs. We are also always dealing with people, and so when we are in a dialogue about an issue, whether in person or online, we should always strive to keep in mind the person over the mere facts of the matter.

Lord Jesus, you are my peace. Help me to communicate your truth with grace, keeping the person, not just the facts, in mind.

One Day at a Time

Although he meant well, one night my husband over-whelmed me by wanting to come up with a plan for what I should be doing to prepare for our postchild-rearing life. But at that moment, I was feeling like several large mountains were blocking my path to tomorrow, much less a life without children at home. So not only did I not want to strategize with him, I could not.

I should have been grateful for his desire to mentally fly me over those mountains to see what it might look like on the other side. Instead, I felt like an ant from which a large protective rock had just been ripped. My thoughts froze, and I wanted to run away and hide.

When I told this to my friend Teresa, she laughed and said, "Oh, I felt that way when our two boys were young and I was smack in the middle of getting my master's degree. My husband was off traveling for work, and so all the housework and child care fell to me at the same time as this intensive course of study. In those days, there was just no more of me to go around. At one point, I remember my mom asking me if I was planning to go on and get my doctorate. That was just too much! I could not even go there with her."

Now, I'm not bad at multitasking, but it was a relief to hear that another woman as sharp as my friend also had a maximum number of activities and thoughts that she could juggle at once. I'm not bad at planning ahead either, but this time I needed to know that it was okay to just put my head down, pray for the strength to put one foot in front of the other, and let the future take care of itself for a while.

It's reassuring to be reminded that God has a plan for our future and that it is a good one (Jeremiah 29:11). I know that this was the truth that my husband was trying to communicate to me, but sometimes in order to maintain our peace, it is also okay to just strap in and ride out the storm.

Lord Jesus, you are my peace. Thank you for the plans you have for me. Give me the peace to plan ahead and trust you day by day.

An Exchange of Goods

With ten children between us, my sister and I used to exchange children's hand-me-down clothing like some women exchange recipes. We were "green" before green was cool. As it happens, the life lessons I learned from exchanging kids' clothing with my sister and with other friends turned out to be quite applicable to sharing advice as well.

With regard to hand-me-downs, I learned to give away only the quality of clothing I hoped to receive. And what I hoped was that the mom transferring that forty-gallon-sized container of clothing from her minivan to mine would have (1) at least washed the clothes; (2) thrown out the torn pants and stained teeshirts; and (3) would not insist on telling my children which of her children had worn that exact same outfit every time we saw her.

With regard to sharing advice, I learned to give only the quality of advice that I hoped to receive. And what I hoped was that the woman would have (1) at least scrubbed the stories clean of unnecessarily personal details; (2) thrown out the names of people and omitted the names of institutions when her advice was based on their failures; and (3) would not feel the need to ask how her advice was working every time we bumped into one another at church, school, or the grocery store.

Basically, I learned that trash is trash and that I should not be passing on anything that isn't worthwhile or does not have value. Just the act of passing it on did not magically bestow added value to it. And even if my advice (or clothing) is beautiful and a perfect fit for the situation, I have chosen to give it away, which means that it is no longer mine but or my friend's to use, to throw away, or to pass on as she sees fit.

When I forget these basic lessons on exchanging advice, it introduces unwanted awkwardness and anxiety into my friendships. Blessed is the woman who can pass on advice as cleanly, thoughtfully, and freely as hand-me-down clothes. She will know peace in her friendships.

Lord Jesus, you are my peace. Teach me how to recognize the "trash" and to exchange only goodness between my family and friends.

It's Not a Competition

The other day my friend Molly was sharing about the social pressure she was feeling to throw an extravagant graduation party for her daughter. I immediately reminded her of what she already knew: that parenting is not a competition. To have peace in her situation, Molly would simply need to cut the music playing in her head and stop the little dance she was doing with her misguided feelings of inadequacy.

Fast-forward about twenty minutes into that same conversation, and I was sharing with Molly how much pressure I was feeling to keep up with the vacation plans of much wealthier family friends. Of course, Molly's advice was the same: "Heidi, cut the music. Stop the dance. Providing for our children is not a competition!"

One of the greatest acts of love and peace we women can do for one another is to stop the rounds of competition. Stop the dance, the race, the showdown—whatever you want to call it.

Instead of reminding one another of the truth that we are more than adequately providing for our children, what if Molly and I had played into each other's competitive desires? What if we had gone online, first to blow her budget on her daughter's party and then to max out my credit cards on some fancy vacation resort? Would feeling as if we were beating out our imagined competition really have given us more peace of mind? Temporarily, maybe. Permanently, absolutely not!

Womanhood is not a competition! We women are different in every way—culturally, economically, intellectually, spiritually, physically, emotionally, and socially—and our families are too. Encouragement rather than competition is what we need to share, because our end goal of eternal happiness is the same. And even for those women who do not share our final heavenly goal, how much more do they need our encouragement in everything they do that is true, right, and beautiful! As that somewhat cheesy bumper sticker says, let's only compete for an "Audience of One"— our Lord.

Lord Jesus, you are my peace. Show me how to encourage rather than to compete with my sisters.

Ordering Our Time

Do you ever have that unsettled feeling that you are in a constant tug-of-war with time? How can we order our time God's way?

My friend Teresa says that as a young mother with a full-time job, she was overwhelmed by the lack of order in her home. "I tried so hard to keep all the toys and baby stuff orderly, but all I really needed was a shovel!" To compensate, she came up with a strict schedule. "With a schedule, now that is where I could impose more order, so I did. I became so driven by my schedule that I really never took the time to cup my babies' faces in my hands and just look at them. I regret that; I really do."

What Teresa shared got me thinking. We don't want a schedule to run us or dictate what we should be doing, but we also don't want to make that the reason we throw out scheduling altogether. In general, I think we can look at a schedule as something to support us in accomplishing the work that God has given us to do. It's like the adventure of turning a house into a home. Disciplined time management is the framework of a house; what we actually do all day (our activities) are the furnishings and decorations.

If we have a structured schedule but we don't fill it with the activities that God has asked us to do, it's as if we are buying a beautifully built house but never bother to furnish or decorate it. Such a life often feels empty, purposeless, and uninviting. Activity is experienced as pure duty.

If we fill our lives with every activity that God could ever want for us but do not have a governing schedule, it's as if we are camping in an open field with every possession we've ever owned scattered all over the place. Such a life often feels like we are drowning in a pile of late fees and good intentions. Time is experienced as perpetual chaos.

However, when we settle ourselves into a life that incorporates solid time management with meaningful activity, life is neither duty nor chaos but more like vacationing in a well-built home that has been tastefully appointed.

Lord Jesus, you are my peace. Help me to order the life you have given me.

Knowledge versus Wisdom

One spring a friend of mine helped me to understand the subtle difference between knowledge and wisdom and how to use that understanding to live a more peaceful life. Sr. Doris and I were good friends because she and her religious sisters hosted a weekly women's Bible study, for which I was one of the discussion leaders. The sisters' convent was associated with our parish community, where my husband and I led the RCIA program. At that time our first child was an infant and still portable, so we felt able to commit to both ministries.

By the next fall, however, my husband had started a new job with a longer commute and more travel, I had gone back to school in the evenings, and we were expecting our second child. Continuing with both ministries suddenly felt like too much, and my peace of mind had flown the coop. The problem was that I didn't want to let anyone down by backing out of either ministry. If we did have to back out, however, I thought that we couldn't leave until someone else had stepped up, and no one else had.

Anguishing over what to do, I spilled my guts to Sr. Doris one day after Bible study. Quietly but assertively (which is how she is), Sr. Doris said this: "Heidi, God does not need you to use all of your capabilities all at once. You and your husband are doing good work, yes, but if you, out of guilt or pride or a mix of both, keep doing something that you feel God is not asking you to do, then you will actually be robbing someone else of the opportunity to do what God is asking them to do. You will be stealing their blessing." Ouch! Her appropriately targeted arrow hit the bull's eye of my prideful heart, and I have never forgotten her godly point.

Miles Kington, a British humorist, wrote this: "Knowledge is knowing that a tomato is a fruit. Wisdom is not putting it in a fruit salad."[10] To help myself recall Sr. Doris's peace-producing advice, I adapted Kington's saying this way: "Knowledge is knowing your talent. Wisdom is knowing the right situation in which to use it."

Lord Jesus, you are my peace. Help me to apply my knowledge wisely.

Increasing and Decreasing

Growing up in northern Wisconsin, I never thought of living on the water as a financial luxury. It was just normal. During the summer months, the lake was what I imagine the shopping mall to be for many teenagers today: a hub of social activity. Our days were spent water skiing, fishing, boating, or just mucking around along the shore.

With cooler temperatures, shorter days, and steam rising from the lake in the early mornings, we knew it was officially time for school to start. Winter brought more social activity, from snowmobiling, snowshoeing, and ice fishing to skating across the vast fields of frozen whiteness. I always hoped that I would not be in school during the few days of late spring when those fields of whiteness turned gray and magically transformed into tinkling ice cubes.

By some comingling of childhood memories and the actual splendor of cool blue waters curving around wooded shorelines, when I am at this lake I feel a surge of peacefulness and contentment. I sense a connection with nature sweeping over me as well as a disconnection from the pressures of my everyday life. I feel gratefully smaller in comparison to the great beauty before me. But then I also feel somehow bigger too, because by some inexplicable means, I sink in and become part of the beauty.

After baptizing Jesus in the Jordan River and acknowledging him as the long-awaited Messiah, John the Baptist said this: "Therefore this joy of mine is now complete. He must increase, but I must decrease" (John 3:29-30). When I read those verses, I feel as if John might have felt that same surge of peacefulness at the Jordan River with Jesus that I feel when I am at the lake.

When or where has your soul found rest by becoming part of a beauty or a truth that is bigger than yourself?

Lord Jesus, you are my peace. Come be the hub of my life. Help me to swim in your greatness by peacefully letting go of my smallness.

The Gift of Tomorrow

My friend Sherry, a university professor, shares how she learned to be grateful for the gift of tomorrow and to make peace with not filling up every minute of every day.

"I am not the same woman that I was just a few years ago. Back then I had a full-time job in administration and four young children at home, and somehow I had decided that it would be a good thing to volunteer to coordinate the university's marching band. I look back and wonder, 'What was I thinking?' Because of all those roles, someone was always knocking on my door—my office door, my front door, my bedroom door—and asking, 'Got a minute?' Well, of course I did! It was my job to have a minute for everyone, but it took its toll.

"One fall, midway through the semester, I found myself in a hotel room madly preparing to give a talk at a conference that I had not even signed up to attend. Looking at my presentation, which I hadn't really had the time to get in order, I knew I was overcommitted—and I was a mess. I remember saying out loud, 'God, something has got to change! I am going to lose my mind.'

"Well, by the end of that semester, everything came skidding to a halt: I was diagnosed with breast cancer. I had to completely surrender my time and my will. From January to May of that spring, I lay in bed trying to recover. I had never had more time on my hands and less control over my life. It was as if God had said, 'Can I have your attention, please? It's your idea of time that has got to change.'

"Today I am much more quickly able to ask myself, 'What really needs to happen here?' and not 'What do I want to have happen?' I don't clutter my days with as many self-imposed obligations because God gives me the gift of tomorrow. I don't think you have to face death in order to appreciate the gift of tomorrow, but after cancer, I am much more at peace with 'today' because I have a whole new appreciation of 'tomorrow.'"

Lord Jesus, you are my peace. Thank you for the gift of tomorrow.

Proclaiming the Gospel

About ten years ago, I was blessed to travel to a Catholic mission outpost in Honduras with two of my teenagers. While we were there, we met a missionary named Jerome. His physical stature and personality resembled the size of his native Texas, but his love for Jesus was even greater. In the years between then and now, Jerome would move across the ocean in order to continue his robust style of evangelization in Africa, marry his Honduran sweetheart, and then return home to work at the diocesan level in his home state.

Jerome's relationship with Jesus is rock solid, and it shows in how peaceful he is when he engages people in faith-based conversations. I especially love how he spins even clichéd questions into opportunities for dialogue. He recently posted a vignette on Facebook that reminded me that not even the toughest questions can rob us of our peace when our faith is anchored in Jesus. Here is what Jerome wrote:

> While I was drinking my coffee yesterday, an Australian man at the hotel where we were holding our convention asked me, "So, mate, you

believe in God and all that stuff?" I said I did, and that my faith in God was my foundation and my hope. "How cute," he said. "Then maybe you can explain why so many children are starving, why there are wars, and why there is general mayhem." I replied, "God asks us the very same question every day."

Brothers and sisters, we truly are the hands and feet of Christ; we bring his love, hope, and message to the world or we don't. It is not a difficult proposal to understand. God has supplied us with enough spiritual and physical tools to construct the type of world that would honor and glorify him. Yet we are a cheeky enough lot to blame him for not doing the work.

I found Jerome's response to the Australian man to be an incredibly disarming answer to the problem of pain and suffering—truthful yet peaceful, compassionate yet empowering. It was a response that I could see myself comfortably pulling out of my own hip pocket and giving to someone who might ask a similar question of me.

Lord Jesus, you are my peace. Give me a heart the size of Texas so that I might truthfully and peacefully proclaim your love.

Go Home and Love Your Family

I have an exquisite black-and-white photo tacked to a bulletin board in my kitchen of a mother and child, along with these words by Blessed Mother Teresa of Calcutta: "What can you do to promote world peace? Go home and love your family."[11] I've had the page pinned up for years because it reminds me that even the little efforts I make at loving the people in my home are worthwhile and part of something bigger.

Something that is easily forgotten in the rush of everyday life is that peace begins with love. Loving others isn't only the calling of missionaries in far-off lands; loving is the universal Christian call, and peace is one of its fruits.

Unfortunately, it has also been rightly observed that it is easier to love the whole world than it is to love the person right in front of us. Why? Because the whole world can't whine for candy at the store, spill milk on the floor, or take the car without asking (and drive it home with an empty gas tank). It is because the sort of love that Mother Teresa talks about is not an ideal that can be neatly filed away in our heads. Instead, it is like a fire that will not stay confined to our hearts.

Mother Teresa treated the poor as people, not problems to be solved. That was her secret: attending to the one person in front of her and not allowing her love for that person to get hijacked by their problems or the societal problems surrounding them.

I try to love like Mother Teresa, and honestly, it drives me a little crazy. I'm much more naturally inclined to want to solve problems, set up programs, and shoo people into line than I am to just sit and be present with someone. But I continue to try, because who can question the worldwide impact of Mother Teresa's style of love? And who doesn't want to be part of the kind of peace that she promoted?

Lord Jesus, you are my peace. Give me a heart for each person who crosses my path today. Help me to love each member of my family.

Trusting Jesus, One Person at a Time

When it comes to promoting peace in the world by loving others the way Mother Teresa of Calcutta told us to love—that is, specifically, generously, and one person at a time—I become acutely aware of my own shortcomings. I sincerely want to love God, my family, and my neighbors. I just, equally sincerely, can't meet all the needs for love that I see around me, and that sometimes puts my soul in an uproar.

Trapped in multiple scheduling webs, I have been known to bellow to my family members and at the same time to frown up at heaven and shout, "Hey, look, I am only one person, okay? I am only one person, and as great as it would be, God has not given me the ability to bilocate. Okay? Okay." Oh, I know that sounds pretty unpeaceful, but my exasperation is not directed at any one person or at God, and by now my family members just laugh at me.

It is in that moment of frustration with my own limits compared to the world's needs that I have thankfully learned to insert a more peaceful response: I pray a short prayer made famous by St. Faustina: "Jesus, I trust in you." So every time I feel overwhelmed by what I can't do for someone I love, I envision placing that person in the Lord's burly arms and praying, "Jesus, I trust in you."

For example, when I would really like to read to my kindergartener before bedtime but also have to go to an evening meeting, I pray, "Jesus, I trust in you; I trust that an older sibling's reading to him instead will show him exactly the right amount of love for today." Or when I would really like to visit an adult child but do not have the time or the finances to pull off a trip, I pray, "Jesus, I trust in you; I trust that my adult child will feel my love for her through a package in the mail, even though I would much rather give her a hug in person."

Even if I can't yet bilocate, Jesus can!

Lord Jesus, you are my peace. Help me to prayerfully entrust into your loving care each member of my family, and instead of being overwhelmed by my limits, let me be in awe of your infiniteness.

Uncharted Territory

The Internet ranks up there with the wheel, the printing press, and electricity as a strong contender for the winner of the most influential human invention of all time. It has drastically altered how we think about, search for, and use information, as well as how we communicate. But has it added to or robbed us of peaceful hearts and minds?

Well, the verdict will be out for many years, but I think it is safe to say that, as it is with any world-changing invention, it is only as positive as the way it is used. Our recent popes have embraced the Internet's positive aspects, robustly encouraging us to get online and engage the culture for Christ in the same way that I imagine medieval popes encouraged people to venture to the New World in order to spread the gospel.

The Internet is, in fact, more like an uncharted wilderness than a benevolent English garden—and we are better off not wandering into unfamiliar territory. As normal as it is to be surfing the Web these days, if we cross over from purposeful use to just loitering online, we are very likely going to get as lost as a missionary sent to the New World without a compass. With social media, especially, addiction is a real risk. In order to assure the highest degree of peace and protection in our online lives, we need to keep the fire of the Holy Spirit burning as brightly in our hearts (and our fingertips) as the pioneers kept their fires burning at their campsites.

Lisa Hendey, creator of the website CatholicMom. com, has this advice: "Just as you wouldn't live in a house without a smoke detector or put your child onto a boat without a life vest, you should never use the Internet without . . . safety provisions."[12]

In order for the Internet to add to our peace of heart and mind, we need to apply Hendey's advice to our own specific situations. We do this by prayerfully asking God to show us where to venture, where not to venture, and how long to linger in this still new electronic frontier.

Lord Jesus, you are my peace. Thank you for the invention of the Internet. Help me to make use of it for your greater glory.

Eyes to See

After accepting my first job outside the home in twenty-four years, I was not thrilled with the fact that I would have to get my kids and myself out the door at the crack of dawn every morning. I was used to the fluid pace of being a full-time parent. Nursing babies, entertaining toddlers, homeschooling, and soccer carpooling had required me to be flexible, but I was the one setting the schedule. Now I wasn't sure if I could again march to the tune of an employer's drum. I think I prayed as hard for help in adjusting to the new schedule as for learning the actual work I had been hired to do.

Then one morning during my new commute, I was wowed by a breathtaking sunrise. A glorious pinky-peach glow was mushrooming across a field and over a distant farm, so I pulled off the road, got out of the car, and waited for the sun to crest over the barn so that I could take a picture. Within a few minutes, a farm truck pulled up and a farmer stared at me through dark sunglasses. I ventured a weak, "Hello?"

"What are you doing here?" he demanded.

Gesturing to the east, I stammered, "I'm taking photographs of that incredible sunrise." Begrudgingly, he looked to where I was pointing, lifted his sunglasses, scoffed, "Aw, for Pete's sake," and then sped off.

Sometimes we are too preoccupied with our own worries to see how God is trying to bless us. The farmer, obviously preoccupied with his early-morning chores and my disturbing presence on his property, had failed to notice that the sky was filled with grandeur that morning. He had eyes, but he did not see (Mark 8:18).

I could relate. In the same way that he had missed the sunrise, I had missed that God would, obviously, help me adjust to my new schedule. And the hope of seeing more sunrises like this one was definitely going to help me get out of the house in the morning!

Lord Jesus, you are my peace. Help me to see the grandeur of your plan for me in every season of my life.

Good Intentions Are Not Enough

We all have a list of things that we know we should be doing but don't actually do. Perhaps it's getting more exercise or eating right. Maybe it's those routine but tedious jobs we need to do periodically to maintain our homes. Whatever it is, so often we feel guilty about not getting to it. And perhaps that is robbing us of our peace at this very moment.

My father used to say, "The road to hell is paved with good intentions." When I was a teenager, he made this sound like a verse from the Bible, invoking its guilt-inducing qualities whenever I tried to give him some lame excuse as to why I hadn't done my chores by Saturday night but still wanted permission to go out with friends.

But Dad was right. When there is a large gap between what we believe (our ideals) and what we do (our actions), we are headed in the wrong direction and our lives lack peace. And the larger the gap, the less peace we experience.

For example, I think having a dog adds warmth and unconditional love to a home, and so it is my ideal to have one. Our puppy has been with us for four months, but her presence is far from ideal because she has accidents everywhere and chews up everything. Good-bye, warmth and unconditional love; hello, outdoor dog pen and "Who let that dog in again?" If only I would take the time to train the dog (the action), I might be able to enjoy the warm fuzziness of a dog at my side (my ideal).

There are times when our ideals need to be adjusted in order for us to live a more peaceful life. It is more often the case, however, that in order to have more peace, we simply need to do what we know we are supposed to do. Or as my dad used to say, we need "to put a little more elbow grease into it."

Lord Jesus, you are my peace. Thank you for walking with me on the road to heaven and for helping me to align both my ideals and my actions in accordance with your will.

Choosing Joy over Happiness

"Look, I just want to be happy, okay! Is that so wrong? Will you just stop with all the religious rules and regulations so that I can just go on my merry way?" That's the plaintive we hear from many in our culture today. Here is Jesus' reply:

> If you keep my commandments, you will abide in my love, just as I have kept my Father's commandments and abide in his love. These things I have spoken to you, that my joy may be in you, and that your joy may be full. This is my commandment, that you love one another as I have loved you. Greater love has no one than this, that someone lay down his life for his friends. You are my friends if you do what I command you. (John 15:10-14)

The truth is that Jesus wants us to be more than just happy. He wants us to be full of joy, because joy begets true inner peace. "Happy" is a shortsighted, here-and-now emotion, like fireworks on the Fourth of July. Most people by their midtwenties have experienced this "pop, flash, and fizzle" type of happiness and have already grown weary of the energy that's needed to manufacture it. Happiness, it turns out, is a nonrenewable resource.

Joy, on the other hand, is not a temporary feeling but a state of being. Joy is like the shimmering rainbow that perpetually hovers over a waterfall. It is something that we did not create nor can we contain. Joy is what we receive when we let the light of Christ shine in, on, and through our life's circumstances. Joy is renewable and gives birth to peace because it is God who generates it, not us. And the key to having joy? Jesus made it simple: "Keep my commandments."

Catholic philosopher and author Peter Kreeft writes this about joy: "Time after time, active willing of God's will, 'Yes' to God, leads out of meaninglessness, passivity, depression, or sorrow into joy. And time after time the pursuit of joy as if it were mine leads to disappointment, emptiness, and restless boredom. . . . Every time we truly say, 'Thy will be done,' we find joy and peace; every time we die, we rise."[13]

Lord Jesus, you are my peace. Give me a greater desire for your joy than for my happiness, and grant me the peace that comes from following your commandments.

A Serenity Prayer

My cleaning spree started with the long-overdue decision to throw out a box of cassette tapes. (You remember those ancestors of the iPod?) It ended four days later with the removal from our house of nine bags of garbage, six bags of donated goods, two ancient computers, one broken TV, and four bins of baby clothes to return to a generous friend. The final result? Four completely cleaned out and newly functional areas of our home.

Phew! No need now to put the house on the market and buy a bigger one!

As I watched the garbage truck pull away with those nine bags, I was riding a wave of cleaning euphoria, daydreaming about what to do with so much reclaimed space. Then my husband asked if I had seen the power cords to the new computer printer that he had just unboxed the day before. Oops.

Continually paring down and organizing our material possessions may feel like a waste of time. It's definitely an ongoing process rather than a one-time project. However, it is one of the best ways to maintain physical peace in our homes. Sometimes, yes, we will unknowingly get rid of something we shouldn't have, but even then, it is easier to deal with the occasional need to replace an item than it is to be constantly shoveling and sifting through piles of stuff no one has needed for years.

I try to push the "reset button" on our stuff once a year, reevaluating what we still need and what we don't. This year I am sorting through preschool toys. Our youngest child is now six years old, but our three oldest children are all over twenty, and so thoughts of grandchildren are beginning to dance in my head. And yet, will any of our low-tech toys even keep the attention of preschoolers five to ten years from now? Or wait—maybe I should have kept those cassette tapes as old-fashioned toys. It's a good thing the trash truck already drove away!

Lord Jesus, you are my peace. Grant me the serenity to keep the material goods I need, the courage to get rid of what I don't need, and the wisdom to know the difference.

Just Imagine

I love children's picture books because they remind us—kids and adults alike—of the power of our imaginations.

"And what," you may ask, "do our imaginations have to do with the virtue of peace?" To which I would answer, "Everything!"

In order to succeed in living the virtue of peace, we must have more than a "head knowledge" of what peace is. We must also be able to feel and imagine what life would be like if it were bathed in Christ's peace.

Once upon a time, back when the countryside of Europe was full of castles, fair maidens, and brave knights on noble steeds, stories of great virtue were often retold through magnificent Catholic art. From dazzling stained-glass windows to expansive murals and powerful sculptures, art was employed by the Church to educate the mostly illiterate laity about the gospel. But it was also used for inspiration, to help people imagine and strive for a life of virtue not always found in the muddy streets and unjust landlords waiting outside the church doors.

Today we have not only art, but also high-quality television shows, movies, and online resources to inspire us. But how often do we use these mediums to merely gather data rather than sparking our imaginations? Using our smartphones only to coordinate our calendars or to follow celebrity gossip, for example, would be like taking shelter from a storm in Notre Dame Cathedral but never looking around to the wonder of where we find ourselves.

Whether it is as a tourist in a cathedral or as a mom reading a children's picture book to a young child, God is reaching out to us. He wants us to feel his peace and to fall in love with the possibility of that peace reigning in all areas of our lives.

So stop the streams of data and worldly "reality" for just a minute and imagine peace reigning on earth. What would that look like?

Lord Jesus, you are my peace. Awaken the power of my imagination. Help me to feel your peace and to fall in love with it.

In Pursuit of Peacefulness

My friend Linda shares what she has learned about her journey to peace.

"I had always thought that it was important to be happy in life. Who doesn't want to be happy? But happiness, I've found, is a temporary state of mind that can come and go with life's daily struggles. What I really desire is interior peace that abides whether I'm feeling happy at the moment or not. And peace is a journey best taken by abandoning myself to God's will. That sounds simple, but it has been the hardest thing I've ever had to do.

"My story, like that of so many others, is full of what I call 'opportunities' from God that have allowed me to grow in holiness. The process of dying to self can be very challenging, and the best 'opportunities' are the ones that have hurt the most. But when I had changed, learned a lesson, or arrived at a point on the other side of the pain or challenging situation, I could say, 'I see why now.' Then I knew that I had used that opportunity to find God's peace.

"Sometimes it takes our inner strength being tested before we learn the greatest lessons. It seems that unless we suffer and are given an opportunity to reach out to God, we often don't. It's just human nature. So suffering really forces us to make that choice to reach out to him. But that's the choice that God wants us to make. It's his will for us to seek him out and to rely on him.

"So I keep asking myself, 'Now, how can I do your will in this situation? How can I grow in holiness?' Because I know that when I seek God's will for my life, I am happy and I have great peace."

Lord Jesus, you are my peace. Guide me through all of life's "opportunities." Help me to do your will so that I can find happiness and peace.

God's Inbox, Our Outbox

My friend Jennifer is a missionary in Africa. Using the analogy of an "outbox" and an "inbox," Jennifer explains how she experiences the peace of God afresh each day.

"Everything that I can't control, I put in an 'outbox,' as the word of God tells us to do: 'Do not be anxious about anything, but in everything by prayer and supplication with thanksgiving let your requests be made known to God. And the peace of God, which surpasses all understanding, will guard your hearts and your minds in Christ Jesus' (Philippians 4:6-7). In the African culture, I have seen examples of strong Christians who ask for everything. Sometimes I am taken aback by how much they ask. They ask people for things. They ask God for things. They don't hold back. And if the answer is 'no,' they accept it quite cheerfully.

"Our American culture teaches us that it is rude to keep asking and that people who ask are not self-reliant and are constantly bothering others for things they should have gotten on their own. But the Lord tells us to pray about everything! I'm starting to realize that my cultural perspective of rudeness has hindered my life of prayer. I've decided to ask for everything. And what's amazing is that I have never in my life had so much peace!

"Of course," Jennifer continued, "the 'inbox' is just as important. The word of God tells us that what we put into and keep in our minds, what we allow to grow or not grow in our thoughts, will, in fact, determine our peace: 'Finally, brothers, whatever is true, whatever is honorable, whatever is just, whatever is pure, whatever is lovely, whatever is commendable, if there is any excellence, if there is anything worthy of praise, think about these things. What you have learned and received and heard and seen in me—practice these things, and the God of peace will be with you' (Philippians 4:8-9).

"A constant inbox of God's word conforms our hearts and minds to his will. Ultimately, our hearts and minds become more like his through the outbox of our prayer and the inbox of his word."

Lord Jesus, you are my peace. Guide me using the "outbox" of prayer and the "inbox" of your holy word as I seek your peace.

Recognizing the Look of Peace

What does peace look like? If we want to be on guard against threats to peace, it might be more effective to learn to recognize what authentic godly peace looks like instead of trying to identify every possible threat to our peace.

Here's a useful analogy. The U.S. Secret Service advises that the best way to guard against counterfeit bills is to become more familiar with United States currency.[14] Knowing what genuine U.S. currency looks like before we ever encounter a counterfeit bill or coin, we are told, is the key to more easily identifying a fake one.

I saw what authentic godly peace looked like when I was helping a friend of mine get ready for a lengthy road trip. She and her husband were supposed to leave that evening, but it was getting past 9:00 p.m. and her husband was still talking to friends. I mentioned that I would have been upset at the delay, but she just grinned and said, "Oh, I've learned that saying heart-felt good-byes is really important to him. Besides, we'll only drive an hour or so tonight, just enough to get out of town." My friend showed me that peace looks like valuing someone else's needs and desires.

Another friend, Karen, discovered authentic godly peace when she was pregnant with her third child. "I remember this time of being wretchedly sick, exhausted, living with my in-laws (who were not Catholic and had only two children), and trying to grapple with why this was God's plan when it made the life of a faith-filled Catholic seem so miserable.

"As I sat there drinking a cup of tea, doing my best to play with my oldest son, I vividly remember coming to the realization that this was not just an unpleasant time to get through; this was God's plan. And if so, then I just needed to say, 'Your will, not mine' (cf. Luke 22:42). I said that phrase over and over until the morning sickness was gone. It gave me a peace that I still feel today."

Repeatedly praying a verse from the Scriptures showed Karen that peace looks like accepting all things, even unpleasant things, as useful and redeemable in God's plan.

To whom or what might you look so that you can recognize authentic godly peace?

Lord Jesus, you are my peace. Help me become an expert at recognizing the look of peace.

Appearances Matter

Women differ in the amount of time and energy they spend taking care of their physical appearance. For example, I rarely get my nails or hair done, but I always shower and get out of my pajamas, even when I am going to be home all day. Why? Because appearances matter.

Taking care of our bodies and our appearance honors God who fashioned our bodies. It shows that we respect ourselves and teaches others to treat us with the same respect. This brings a sense of peace to our relationships, because how we care for ourselves and how we dress communicate what we believe and set the ground rules for our interactions with others.

For Christians, an important element of that message is modesty. As one catechist wrote,

Modesty protects the beauty and dignity of the body while keeping the focus on the whole person. . . . When we live the virtue of modesty, we set the tone of our relationships. People in our company are then careful how they dress, act, and speak, being careful of subject matter, avoiding "dirty jokes" or swearing. Our developed virtue of modesty ensures an appropriate and wholesome manner of speaking.[15]

Another point to consider, from Catholic author and chastity speaker Jason Evert, concerns modesty and its effect on male/female relationships:

Without a word, modesty invites men to realize that women have more to offer than just their bodies. . . . When the woman veils her body with modest clothing, she is not hiding herself from men. On the contrary, she's revealing her dignity to them. As a result, the man is free to take her seriously as a woman.[16]

What could you do to improve the messages you are sending to others about your beauty and personal dignity? How could you take better care of the incredible body God has given you and thereby enjoy more peace in your relationships?

Lord Jesus, you are my peace. Help me to set a tone of respect and peace in my relationships by the way I care for myself and dress.

What's So Funny?

Humor is important for maintaining a peaceful disposition while coping with life's ups and downs. I was reminded of that one day last winter while trying to get to school with my kindergartener.

We were late pulling into the parking lot because of an overnight snowstorm and had to rush to make it into the building by the first bell. Because I am a faculty member of the school, I was desperately trying to keep up professional appearances as my son and I scurried in front of a line of moms in minivans, with me dodging snow banks in my high heels and him stomping right through them in his older sibling's boots. Then my son darted ahead of me into the crosswalk, and the packages in my arms started to slip. It looked increasingly like a disaster waiting to happen.

As we approached the front door, I clumsily tried to free up even one finger to push the buzzer to be let in. Thankfully, a man in a gray three-piece suit was leaving the building just as we had arrived, and he held the door open for us. As I opened my mouth to offer some token of gratitude, he put out his hand and said, "That will be five dollars, please."

The ceremonial "thank you" froze on my lips and a genuine laugh burst forth. I had anticipated a clever remark about faculty kids running free in traffic or "certainly having my hands full," but not simple good humor. It made my day.

When job interviewers ask that perpetually tricky question, "What is your biggest weakness?" my stock answer is that I often take life too seriously. I need to add laughter to my everyday life like Scandinavians need light therapy in the winter. Laughter brightens everything! It lightens the same old facts, features, and routines of life and predisposes us to being more peaceful and less likely to react negatively even when things don't go exactly as planned.

If you are comedy-challenged like me, you can make some deliberate choices to lighten up. Perhaps you could watch some clean funny movies, subscribe to jokes on your mobile device, get a joke-a-day calendar—or just hang out with funny friends.

Lord Jesus, you are my peace. Lighten my days with humor so that I will be more at peace.

A Litany of Trust

Do you have a litany of regrets?

I wish . . .
that I hadn't bought a house
that I had bought a house
that I hadn't worked outside the home
that I had worked outside the home
that I had gone to college
that I hadn't gone into debt so I could go to college
that I had gotten married
that I hadn't gotten married so young
that I had had children
that I had had children when I was younger
. . . because then I would not be in this predicament.

We need to abandon such litanies and their guilt-laden trajectories. They are of no use to our pursuit of peace for today or for the future. We can, instead, recite a peace-filled and scripturally based litany of trust that reads more like this:

I trust . . .

that you, Lord God, can work all things together for my good (Romans 8:28)

that you, Lord God, have forgiven all my trespasses (Romans 8:1-4)

that in your time, Lord God, all things will be made new (Revelation 21:5)

that you, Lord God, Creator of heaven and earth, love me (Psalm 146:6 and John 3:16)

that you, Lord God, know all the details of my situation (Luke 12:7)

that you, Lord God, are preparing a place for me in heaven (John 14:3)

that you, Lord God, have been with me all along (2 Timothy 1:14)

that you, Lord, God, are trustworthy (1 Timothy 1:15)

that you, Lord God, want to have fellowship with me (John 17:6-12)

that you, Lord God, want me to have joy (John 17:13-19)

. . . because your holy word says it is true.

Lord Jesus, you are my peace. Guard my thoughts today. Help me to move past my regrets and steep my thoughts in your word.

Financial Peace

Most of us can probably relate to the milkman Tevye in the musical *Fiddler on the Roof*. Tevye accepts his station in life, but he also inquires of God, "Would it spoil some vast eternal plan if I were a wealthy man?" Who hasn't asked that question in the middle of balancing the budget!

When it comes to having financial peace, however, nothing beats the surefire plan of living within one's means. I know it's hard to do in our age of never-ending lines of credit, but here are some of the strategies I use for living within my means:

❧ Don't wait until you have an actual or online shopping cart full of items to pray for the willpower to say no. Pray for the ability to say no to shopping itself, and then even when you are shopping, pray for the grace not to desire unaffordable items.

❧ Don't lead yourself into temptation by keeping sales flyers and catalogs around the house. Take them straight from the mailbox to the recycling bin. Also, do not invite temptation by spending your leisure time at the mall or on retailers' websites if you do not have money to spend.

🕉 If you do splurge, choose how much you will spend before heading to the stores, get that amount in cash, and leave your credit and debit cards at home. Maximize your splurge by going to secondhand stores where your cash will go a lot further.

When I am tempted to buy things I can't afford, I ask myself this question: "Which do I want more, this item or financial peace?" This reminds me that by not spending money I do not have, I am actually "buying" financial peace for me and my family. It takes ongoing and deliberate effort to not be "led into temptation" when it comes to materialism, but the resulting financial peace is well worth the effort.

If you have other ideas for living within your means, please share them with your friends. Each of us needs all the help we can get!

Lord Jesus, you are my peace. Grant me the grace to live within my means.

The Gift of Gratitude

The summer my dad passed away was a tough time for me. I had already been on edge emotionally about sending our fourth child off to college, and she was only going to be three hours away! With little warning, Dad was now an eternity away, and the peace of his being nearby, even in his declining health, was lost forever.

I was with my dad the day before he died. The last thing I did for him was to bring him a piece of home-made strawberry-rhubarb pie, and the last thing he said to me was "Thank you." I hugged him and told him I'd be back to see him in two days with our youngest child so that he could play Legos with his grandpa. "Thank you," Dad had whispered.

The last months of helping Mom care for Dad had been filled with many such thank-yous. "Thank you for taking me and my sister to dinner." "Thank you for taking me fishing on Father's Day." "Thank you for leaving me a voice mail." He thanked us for things that were really nothing—common courtesies at best—but his gratitude came from the bottom of his heart.

Dad had encouraged me my whole life, but especially at the end, when he made it his mission. One of the last text messages he sent was to congratulate my sixteen-year-old son on winning a high school track award. One of his last outings was to cheer for my eighteen-year-old daughter at her final high school soccer game. One of his last e-mails was an offer to contribute some cash to help my oldest son get to that year's Super Bowl game.

What lessons about peace did my dad leave me by his actions? He demonstrated that even during the most trying of times, showing gratitude and offering small intentional acts of encouragement can make the world a more peaceful, gentler place to live.

Thank you, Dad.

Lord Jesus, you are my peace. Let me be an example of gratitude and encouragement to others.

Our Ultimate Desire

On an intellectual level, we know that material things cannot satisfy our need for personal worth and esteem. We also know that money cannot buy us love or happiness, nor can material possessions even come close to satisfying our deepest desire, which is a meaningful relationship with God. And yet on an emotional level, don't we just love getting something new or opening a birthday card and finding cash inside? Doesn't "retail therapy" actually make us feel better, if only temporarily? So what's going on here?

It is true that we will come up short anytime we try to put material things or money in the place of God. The same will happen if we try to substitute mere recreation or hobbies for Christian service or prayer. However, it is also true that these lesser goods do slake our thirst for love and meaning to some degree. Unfortunately, it's this little taste of satisfaction that can cause us to desire more of what is ultimately unable to wholly satisfy us, leaving us vulnerable to restlessness, discontentment, and a lack of peace. The Christian apologist C. S. Lewis put it this way:

It would seem that Our Lord finds our desires not too strong, but too weak. We are half-hearted creatures, fooling about with drink and sex and ambition when infinite joy is offered us, like an ignorant child who wants to go on making mud pies in a slum because he cannot imagine what is meant by the offer of a holiday at the sea. We are far too easily pleased.[17]

What I love about Lewis' analogy is that it puts the things of this world and the things of the next on a comparative scale instead of a competitive one. It acknowledges that the riches of this world and our desire for them are not all bad or in opposition to the riches of the next world. Rather, they are more often simply less than what the next world has to offer: a sip of fruit juice compared to a goblet of wine. It helps me remember that it is God that I really want when I am tempted, yet again, to buy something I really don't need.

Lord Jesus, you are my peace. Help me not be so easily pleased with the lesser goods of this world but to hold out for the greater goods of heaven.

Love Wants Union

While giving a talk on the power of intercessory prayer, author and speaker Sr. Ann Shields, SGL, said this: "Love wants union."[18] In the vast seashore of ideas about love, this single statement suddenly stood out to me. It was like an exquisite seashell begging to be picked out of the sand and carefully taken home in my pocket. Sensing that the statement was a pearl of great wisdom about peace, I thought more about what it really means and what it implies for our lives in Christ.

On a theological level, "love wants union" summarizes John 3:16: "For God so loved the world, that he gave his only Son, that whoever believes in him should not perish but have eternal life." Our eternal union with God is the highest purpose of his love for us, as revealed in the life, death, and resurrection of Jesus Christ. We will know no greater peace than when we have what true love wants, and that is perfect union with God.

But on this side of heaven, as well as on a very practical level, we can use "love wants union" as a marvelous guiding motto. It can guide the big picture of our prayer life as we commit to praying for unity within our Church, for unity among Christian denominations, and for unity among all people of good will.

It can also guide our interpersonal relationships. For example, I have my most peaceful and productive conversations when I remember to ask myself this question in advance of talking to someone: "What approach to this topic will bring about the most unity between us?"

It's not that every word or action of ours will be capable of achieving union on its own. But just as a beach is the sum of a great multitude of grains of sand, so it is that peace on earth is the sum of a great multitude of prayers and actions that are oriented toward the desire for loving union with God and neighbor.

Lord Jesus, you are my peace. Let my words and deeds be guided by the desire for union with you and with my neighbor so that we all may know peace.

Examining the Reasons That We Work

Deciding whether or not to take a break from employment after having children remains one of the most distressing choices a mom has to make. Fortunately, many places of employment have become a lot more flexible for moms and dads alike. But when we choose to keep up our employable skills at the same time that we also want to enjoy a stable, peaceful marriage and family life, we must examine our reasons carefully. If our motives are wrong, we may lack peace but be hard-pressed to understand why.

One of the most overwhelmingly positive and peace-filled reasons for a wife and mother to keep up her employable skills is because she is an individual uniquely gifted by God, someone who has gifts and talents outside of nurturing a family. For this reason, she should value herself enough to explore and expand her interests and talents, whether or not they result in a paycheck. Another reason for a wife and mother to continue paid employment—and probably the most practical one— is so that she can contribute to the family's finances.

On occasion I will read a magazine or online article on the topic that really disturbs me because it suggests that no wife is immune to abandonment by her spouse, and therefore every woman must work, even if she has young children, in order to protect herself. This advice is based on fear and does not bring peace to either spouse.

When we choose to say yes to marriage, then by authentic Catholic teaching we also choose to say yes to being other-centered. Both husband and wife freely choose that all the skills, talents, and resources that they have previously managed for their own benefit will now be put at the disposal of one another and the children that are the fruit of their union (*Catechism of the Catholic Church*, 1601).

If we did not approach marriage and family from this angle in the beginning, it is never too late to correct our course.

Lord Jesus, you are my peace. Thank you for creating me rich in talents and abilities. Give me the peace that comes with offering these for the good of others, regardless of my state in life.

Choosing Peace, Not Power

I encountered a situation recently in which I had to choose between two worldly proverbs: "Knowledge is power" and "Ignorance is bliss." Normally, I'm the kind of gal who opts for knowledge, but in this case, knowledge was also poison.

The situation involved a particularly difficult person who had become verbally aggressive. I had set up a filter to delete e-mails from this person, but somehow a message appeared in my inbox anyway, and so I had to make a choice.

I could open the e-mail and read for myself just how unhealthy this person's thinking was. Knowing what had been written would give me power because I could say to anyone questioning the charity of my behavior, "See? This is how this person treats me, even if this person is as sweet as pie to you." In order to get that power, however, I would have to read this person's words, thereby allowing them to seep into my mind and heart and unalterably poison my attitude.

Or I could concede that enough was enough, permanently delete the e-mail, and just let it go. In the end, the peaceable choice was clear. I clicked on the "delete" button.

From time to time, we will encounter intentionally hurtful people—people who send insulting e-mails or worse. To help myself deal with such people, I've learned to separate them from their unkind actions by envisioning the unkindness as a cup of poison set in front of me. It makes no difference why the cup was set before me, who placed it there, or if anyone else thinks that the drink is poisonous. I do not have to drink from a cup of poison. By the grace of God, I can choose real peace over power and simply walk away.

Lord Jesus, you are my peace. Help me to resist the temptation to have power over others. I choose to live in peace. Help me be merciful, and protect me from anyone who would seek to injure me.

Peace in Parenting

I've been preparing a digital photo album to give to our daughter when she graduates from high school. Talk about emotional! I know that it is the eighteen-year-old version of my impish beauty that will stroll into the house after school today. But if I close my eyes, any one of the little pixies pictured in this album could bounce into the room, and it would feel completely normal.

This is our fourth child to graduate from high school and move on to college, and it is not any easier with her than it was with her older siblings. What mother is ever ready to let a child leave the nest? As I scan through the pictures of my daughter's childhood, however, I have deep peace.

I have peace not because her childhood was perfect, nor because I have been the ideal mom. Far from it. I have peace because I know that I did my best to love her for who God made her to be and that I took seriously the charge given to me at her baptism to bring her up in the practice of the faith.

The truth is that there is no one set way to parent a child so that he or she will turn out to be perfectly happy, holy, and capable. I wish there were. But with a seemingly wry sense of humor, God gave our children the same free will that he gave to us. This doesn't have to rob us of our peace, however. In fact, it is just the opposite.

When we dedicate ourselves to discerning and discovering how God wants us to parent and then commit ourselves to doing it, we can have peace. If we continually ask for the help of the Holy Spirit as we wind our way along the path of parenting, we can have peace, even if the end result doesn't look like what we might have envisioned. If we can honestly say that we have exhausted ourselves for the Lord and for the children he entrusted to our care, then we can go to bed and sleep in peace.

Lord Jesus, you are my peace. I thank you for your help as I continue on this parenting journey.

Power in Weakness

One of the most empowering gifts of peace we can give to each other is to confess our weaknesses. It feels counterintuitive, but as St. Paul writes, in God's economy admitting our weaknesses is actually better than admitting our strengths: "But he said to me, 'My grace is sufficient for you, for my power is made perfect in weakness.' Therefore I will boast all the more gladly of my weaknesses, so that the power of Christ may rest upon me." (2 Corinthians 12:9).

My friend Theresa shares how confessing her tendency to be impatient has helped her. "I periodically lose my patience and my peace when dealing with my children—certain ones, especially. Having a husband who is mindful of my weakness helps me manage my response to those children." The result of Theresa's being humble enough to admit her weakness to her husband is that she empowers him to get more involved in parenting. And that, of course, allows the power of Christ to dwell more richly in the whole family.

Theresa concludes, "Humility is important in keeping your peace: knowing who you are before God, knowing your limitations, knowing when to step out in faith despite your limitations, accepting failure, and accepting other people's failures too."

It is not natural for most of us to admit, much less to boast about, our weaknesses, as St. Paul advises that we do. When my husband and I were first married, I might hold out for days before apologizing for my part in an argument because I was just too stubborn to admit that I, too, might have contributed to whatever the problem was. Learning to unmask rather than to hide behind my stubbornness, however, has created a much more peaceful and humble relationship between my husband and me. I have found that the pleasure of fewer and less intense arguments is well worth the pain of disclosing my weaknesses or faults.

There is nothing quite as disarming as someone who sincerely admits his or her own weakness and apologizes for its negative impact on the situation. And so, as unlikely as it may seem, honestly admitting weakness can bring empowering peace.

Lord Jesus, you are my strength. Free me to accept my weaknesses so that your power and your peace might dwell more richly in me and in my relationships.

The Healer of Hearts

Sometimes when we are lacking emotional peace, we don't immediately realize the source of our sorrow or anxiety. But then someone speaks unexpected words of healing, and a rain cloud of tears bursts forth. This happened to me when I received the following two compliments within days of each other.

"You have such a beautiful family," said a petite grandma when my four-year-old opened the door for her out of the church. And then, in an end-of-the-year e-mail exchange, the chaplain of my teenagers' new high school signed off with this: "God bless you and your wonderful family."

Why did both of these compliments make me burst into tears? Because having moved two years earlier, we no longer had friends who knew all of our children or who had interacted with us as an entire family. When we moved, the oldest two children were already in college, the third oldest followed her older siblings only eighteen months later, and the three youngest, although at home, were not initially in the same schools. All this meant that being known as a family, as "the Brattons," was no longer a thing.

I had no idea how much I was grieving the loss of being known as a family until receiving those two unsolicited compliments. I am positive that neither of these people knew the healing impact of what they had communicated, but their words marked a turning point in God's healing of the residual emotional wounds of moving.

Are you anxious or hurting today? Maybe you don't even know why, but you haven't felt like yourself lately. It's okay. Even if you don't know the origin of your emotional pain, God does, and he wants to heal you. If God can mend a heart like mine, which I came to realize was shattered into a thousand little pieces and scattered along the road we had left behind when we moved, he can and will do the same for yours. God wants to bring you back to life and can do it even without your complete understanding. Trust in God to restore your peace. Listen for his words spoken through others. Read his words of comfort in the Bible, and rest in his love.

Lord Jesus, you are my peace. Please, heal my wounds, bring me back to life, and restore me to wholeness.

Authentic Beauty

Late one afternoon I found myself standing in the cosmetic aisle of a local pharmacy. The men's products, packaged in navy blue and hunter green, were on one side. The women's products, packaged in bright pink and lime green, were on the other. I was searching for hair dye #9 because my stylist had mentioned that it might hide the unwanted gray starting to poke out of my light brown hair.

As I stood there befuddled by the array of choices, a young girl and her father joined me. He was focused on the side of the aisle with the men's products; she was fascinated by the other side for women. After a short time, she pulled a box off the shelf and exclaimed, "Here it is! This is the color I want my hair to be, Daddy!"

"What?" responded the dad without shifting his gaze. "What do you mean? I like the color you have the best."

I smiled and glanced over to see what color the little girl's hair was. I smiled even wider when I saw precious light brown pigtails poking out beneath a pink baseball cap. With his almost absentminded response, this father had given his daughter one of the greatest gifts she would ever receive: peace with her physical appearance and the assurance that his love did not depend on her outer beauty. What woman isn't starving for that kind of peace and assurance?

We feminine creatures can get pretty fixated on our exterior beauty, but there is only one beauty tip we really need to know: authentic beauty radiates from within. Every other kind of beauty—hair, makeup, or wardrobe choices—is just window dressing with which we can have fun but on which we cannot hang our true worth.

"It's important that you understand that your worth is not found in perfect skin, lovely dresses, or a delicate figure—all of which can be lost with time," writes Laura Jachimowicz in an article about the things we need to teach our daughters. "Rather, your advantage lies in the millions of qualities that no photo or mirror will ever capture."[19]

Putting back hair dye #9, which by then I had located, I smiled at the man and said, "That was exactly the right response, Dad. Way to go."

Lord Jesus, you are my peace. Wrap me in your fatherly love and grant me the peace that comes with accepting myself exactly as you created me to be.

Speaking the Truth in Love

What do we say or do in a relationship when there seems to be an inescapable tension between what is logical or truthful speech and what is loving or compassionate speech? In other words, is it possible to speak a hard truth in a peaceful way? For example, what do we say when a co-worker continually gossips? Or when a friend asks to borrow money yet again when she hasn't yet paid us back from an earlier loan?

This tension presents itself in more touchy areas of life as well. For example, what do we say to a friend who gleefully announces that she is moving in with her boyfriend? Understanding and learning to apply the biblical phrase "speaking the truth in love" (Ephesians 4:15) can help us to have peace in responding to these situations.

For beginners, the phrase "speaking the truth in love" does not mean saying or doing whatever true thing we want to say or do as long as we say or do it sweetly. And it doesn't mean not speaking the truth because it might be perceived by the other person as unloving. The key to understanding the phrase lies in its use of the preposition "in." Authentic godly truth is informed by, infused with, or immersed in love. When we speak out of this type of truth, it is felt very differently by people than is truth that is spoken over, under, or even alongside love.

So what might it look like to speak truth that is informed and immersed in love? It might look like bringing to your co-worker's attention the results of her gossip. It might look like not loaning your friend money but paying her part of the bill on a lunch date. It might look like visiting your friend and her live-in boyfriend but not staying at their home.

The atmosphere created by speaking (or acting out of) truth in love is one of empathetic engagement on some meaningful level. It is an atmosphere marked by peace.

Lord Jesus, you are my peace. Teach me how to speak the truth in love.

In the Shadow of His Wings

This month has felt like it will never end. I am over-loaded, and I knew I would be. I'm the one who agreed to the deal, but agreeing hasn't made it any easier. Perhaps you also have been a finalist in the reality show I've nicknamed *The Race to Run Up the Steepest Face of a Forty-Story Sand Dune in Flip-Flops in the Blistering Sun with Multiple Unzipped Backpacks Overflowing with Unrealistic Expectations from Home, Work, School, and Extended Family*.

Okay, so the title needs a little work, but I think you get where I'm going with it. In this reality show, I am one of the last remaining contestants, and if the sand weren't so blazing hot, I would totally let myself fall and never get up. I've lost my competitive edge.

Does your life ever feel like a real-life drama in which exhaustion is the principal adversary? Some craziness is of our own choosing, but even if we thought we knew what we were getting into, we might need to reassess our chosen path and adjust or even drop some of our load. Other times craziness just descends upon us like locusts from the sky, swarming and chewing up all our good intentions and reserves. What can we do?

We can seek the Lord in prayer by imitating the example of King David in the Old Testament, who from a cave cried out, "Be merciful to me, O God, be merciful to me, / for in you my soul takes refuge; / in the shadow of your wings I will take refuge, / till the storms of destruction pass by" (Psalm 57:1).

When we turn to God in prayer, his peace casts a soothing shadow over our lives like the wings of a mother dove returning to her nest. No matter what "reality" we find ourselves in, the peace of Christ is our refuge. Through prayer we can join King David in proclaiming, "For you have been my help, / and in the shadow of your wings I will sing for joy" (Psalm 63:7).

Lord Jesus, you are my peace. Shelter me in the shadow of your wings. Be my refuge from the scorching effects of busyness and the uninvited swarms of anxiety.

Peace with Mother Church

Switching to a different parish can be a traumatic experience, whatever the reason. The transition can be made more peaceful, however, if we bear in mind that just as individual people have different personalities with diverse strengths and weaknesses, so do individual Catholic parishes. If we have prayerfully decided that we cannot remain peaceful in a particular parish, we do not have to reject the entire Catholic Church. The universal Church is way bigger than the people or the programs in any single parish community. The *Catechism of the Catholic Church* describes it like this:

> In Christian usage, the word "church" designates the liturgical assembly, but also the local community or the whole universal community of believers. These three meanings are inseparable. "The Church" is the People that God gathers in the whole world. She exists in local communities and is made real as a liturgical, above all a Eucharistic, assembly. She draws her life from the word and the Body of Christ and so herself becomes Christ's Body. (752)

Here is one analogy that works for me. Just as a mother cat supplies the same milk for each of her kittens, our Mother Church supplies the same liturgical grace to each believer in Christ. We are fed simultaneously but through different parish communities.

This helps me see that changing parishes is not as big a deal as it may feel at the time, no matter what the reason for changing might be. It diffuses the matter into one of simple repositioning instead of rejecting, like a kitten latching on at a different place on the very same mamma cat to receive the very same nutrients. Even more important, it provides a very peaceful and reasoned approach to a potentially traumatic event.

Lord Jesus, you are my peace. Thank you for my local parish and for keeping each of us in the community connected to the universal Church through your word and the sacraments.

A Treasure beyond Compare

The worth of knowing God's peace is immeasurable. To better understand this worth, we can meditate on peace as it is revealed to us in Sacred Scripture. Pray for the Holy Spirit to inspire you, and then read the following verses slowly. As you read, look first for the common denominators of peace and then for its distinctive characteristics:

- "Peace I leave with you; my peace I give to you. Not as the world gives do I give to you. Let not your hearts be troubled, neither let them be afraid." (John 14:27)
- Therefore, since we have been justified by faith, we have peace with God through our Lord Jesus Christ. (Romans 5:1)
- And let the peace of Christ rule in your hearts, to which indeed you were called in one body. And be thankful. (Colossians 3:15)
- The LORD sits enthroned as king forever. / May the LORD give strength to his people! / May the LORD bless his people with peace! (Psalm 29:10-11)

One common denominator that I found is that peace belongs to God. Peace is God's property and possession. Another is that peace is effectual. It accomplishes something good in the lives of those who have it. Here are some distinctive characteristics of peace that I noticed:

🌀 Peace exists in two forms, heavenly and worldly. Heavenly peace can be given by God to us on earth and is accompanied by a lack of trouble and fear.

🌀 Peace is the result of a faith-filled response to the gospel. Peace with God is available and secured through a relationship with Jesus Christ.

🌀 Peace has the ability to govern our lives and the power to call disparate parts into a unified purpose.

🌀 Peace is authoritative; those to whom it is given are compelled to express their gratitude.

🌀 Peace is a blessing that is accompanied by strength. Peace belongs to God. Those people to whom he has given it are his own people.

Even this short meditation reveals that God's peace is much like a beautiful gem whose many different facets contribute to the beauty of the whole.

Lord Jesus, you are my peace. Open my heart to the many facets of your peace.

ENDNOTES

1. Maya Angelou, "Maya on Oprah," Vibrant Word (blog), accessed August 10, 2014, http://www.vibrantword.com/maya_angelou.html.

2. Pope Francis, *Evangelii Gaudium*, 39, 44.

3. Pope Francis, *Evangelii Gaudium*, 7, 10.

4. Matthew Kelly, *Rediscover Catholicism* (Cincinnati OH: Beacon Publishing, 2010), 160, 163.

5. Commonly attributed to Lily Tomlin in *People* magazine (December 26, 1977).

6. Ramsey, Dave, *Complete Guide to Money* (Brentwood: Lampo Press, 2011), 27.

7. Pope Francis, Homily, October 13, 2013, accessed October 17, 2014 at http://w2.vatican.va/content/francesco/en/homilies/2013/documents/papa-francesco_20131013_omelia-giornata-mariana.html.

8. St. Teresa of Avila, "Saint Teresa of Avila Prayer," Big Catholics (blog), accessed February 28, 2014, http://www.bigccatholics.com/2012/06/saint-teresa-of-avila-prayer.html.

9. Donna Boucher, "What Matters," Quiet Life (blog), May 14, 2014, http://booshay.blogspot.com/2014/05/what-matters.html?spref=fb.

10. Andy McSmith, "Fond Farewell to the Genius of Miles Kington," *The Independent*, February 12, 2008, accessed October 21, 2014, http://www.independent.co.uk/news/uk/this-britain/fond-farewell-to-the-genius-of-miles-kington-781024.html.

11. "Biography Mother Teresa," quote from interview at Nobel Peace Prize Ceremony, 1979, Biography Online (blog), accessed January 13, 2014, http://www.biographyonline.net/nobelprize/mother_teresa.html.

12. Lisa Hendey, *The Handbook for Catholic Moms* (Notre Dame, IN: Ave Maria Press, 2010), 122.

13. Peter Kreeft, *Heaven, the Heart's Deepest Longing* (San Francisco: Ignatius Press, 1989), 158.

14. United States Secret Service, "Know Your Money," United States Secret Service (web page), accessed October 19, 2014, http://www.secretservice.gov/money_detect.shtml.

15. Office of Catechesis & Evangelization and Catholic Schools, Diocese of La Crosse, WI, "Virtue of the Month," Diocese of La Crosse (website), accessed August 10, 2014, http://www.dioceseoflacrosse.com/ministry_resources/catechesis/files/Modesty_Teacher.pdf.

16. Jason Evert, "Modesty, What's the Point?" Catholic Answers Chastity Outreach (blog), June 2, 2014, http://chastity.com/article/modesty-what%E2%80%99s-the-point.

17. C. S. Lewis, *The Weight of Glory* (New York: HarperOne, 2009), 26.

18. Sr. Ann Shields, SGL, from a talk given at the Mothers' Tea at Spiritus Sanctus Academy, Plymouth, MI, May 7, 2014.

19. Laura Jachimowicz, "5 Things Every Daughter Should be Taught," *Verily* (online magazine), accessed June 13, 2014, http://verilymag.com/5-things-every-daughter-should-be-taught/#comment-26141.

the WORD among us ®
The Spirit of Catholic Living

This book was published by The Word Among Us. Since 1981, The Word Among Us has been answering the call of the Second Vatican Council to help Catholic laypeople encounter Christ in the Scriptures.

The name of our company comes from the prologue to the Gospel of John and reflects the vision and purpose of all of our publications: to be an instrument of the Spirit, whose desire is to manifest Jesus' presence in and to the children of God. In this way, we hope to contribute to the Church's ongoing mission of proclaiming the gospel to the world so that all people know the love and mercy of our Lord and grow more deeply in their faith as missionary disciples.

Our monthly devotional magazine, *The Word Among Us*, features meditations on the daily and Sunday Mass readings, and currently reaches more than one million Catholics in North America and another half million Catholics in one hundred countries around the world. Our book division, The Word Among Us Press, publishes numerous books, Bible studies, and pamphlets that help Catholics grow in their faith.

To learn more about who we are and what we publish, log on to our website at www.wau.org. There you will find a variety of Catholic resources that will help you grow in your faith.

Embrace His Word, Listen to God . . .

www.wau.org